EARLY RECOLLECTIONS
AND LIFE OF
DR. JAMES STILL

1812-1885

RUTGERS UNIVERSITY PRESS
New Brunswick, New Jersey

Library of Congress Cataloging in Publication Data

Still, James, 1812–1885.
Early recollections and life of Dr. James Still,
1812–1885.

Reprint of the ed. published by Lippincott, Phila-
delphia.
1. Still, James, 1812–1885. 2. Negro physicians—
Correspondence, reminiscences, etc. I. Title.
[DNLM: 1. History of medicine—Biology. WZ100
S8573e 1877F]
R154.S8348A33 1973   616'.0092'4 [B]   73-14624
ISBN 0-8135-0769-3

© 1971 by Medford Historical Society
© 1973 by Rutgers University—The State University
of New Jersey

Publisher's Note

Levin and Charity Still were slaves in Maryland prior to moving to Indian Mills, New Jersey, where James Still was born on April 9, 1812. In this autobiography James says that his mother "claimed" she had eighteen children. He names only nine, and it is possible that he never saw his other brothers and sisters, who were placed with families that could support them.

James was not the first member of the family to write a book. In 1856 his brother Peter published *The Kidnapped and the Ransomed*, the story of the attempt to free his wife and children, who were slaves in Alabama.

In 1872 James's younger brother William published a book about his experiences—*The Underground Rail Road*. He sheltered the wife and children of John Brown while Brown was awaiting execution and later became an official of numerous philanthropic organizations. He published two more books—*Voting and Laboring* and *Struggle for the Rights of the Colored People of Philadelphia*.

In her Historical Sketch, Margery Cridland gives a brief account of the discovery of James Still's book in 1930 and how it came to the attention of the Medford Historical Society, which reprinted it in 1971.

Additional details about James Still, his family, and his book can be found in *Forgotten Towns of Southern New Jersey* and *The Roads of Home* by Henry Charlton Beck, published by Rutgers University Press.

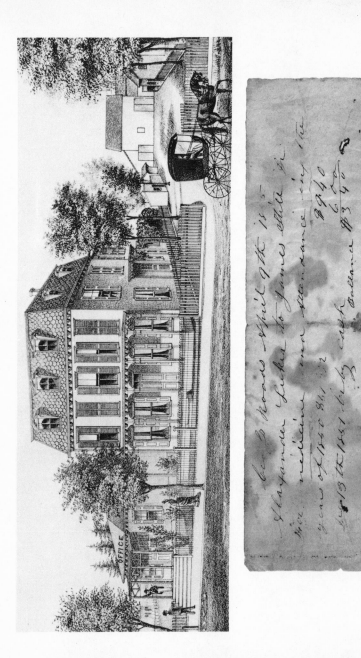

Historical Sketch

Known in the Medford area as "doctor," James Still was not a licensed physician. The title was conferred by grateful patients who welcomed his gentle remedies after the "heroic" treatment prescribed by most nineteenth-century doctors. Purging and blood-letting were common practice and medication was intended to produce violent results. Blisters, cupping, leeches, and tobacco injections were still used.

No wonder suffering patients preferred the vegetable preparations and cooling liniments of Dr. Still. It is possible that many of his "cures" can be credited to the lack of heroic remedies rather than the treatment itself. A medical report of 1863 states: "A number of physicians were invited to see this case . . . whose suggestions were eagerly listened to, and . . . acted upon. Having exhausted our armamentarium, the case was abandoned to nature; a general improvement took place, and the girl is now comparatively well."

From childhood James Still dreamed of becoming a doctor but did not consider himself qualified with only three months' schooling. However, he wanted "to go at something better than work by the day," (p. 70) so he began to distill roots and herbs selling them to druggists in Philadelphia. Encouraged by a Quaker gentleman who asked, "Has thee a notion of studying medical botany?" (p. 72), he purchased some books and began learn-

Page numbers in parentheses refer to *Early Recollections and Life of Dr. James Still*. Unless otherwise noted, all other quotations and the medical information are from *Medicine and Health in New Jersey: A History* by David L. Cowen, originally published by Van Nostrand Company, Princeton, N.J., in 1964, now distributed by Rutgers University Press.

ing about medicine. Neighbors asked for his remedies, and soon he was going through the country in a homemade wagon with a cigar-box for a medicine-chest, healing the sick. He wrote: "It did not occur to me at this time, however, that I was practising medicine. I thought that I was but doing a friendly service to a fellow-being." (p. 77)

Times were ripe for practitioners such as Dr. Still. Medicine was in transition, and doctors were questioning the use of massive doses of drugs such as calomel and opium. Dr. R. H. Page of Burlington County wrote in the *Country Practitioner:* "veratrum viridi has filled many a grave; hydrate of chloral hushed many a victim; chloroform a holocaust of death, and the thousand and one recommendations that appear of knock-down, drag-out doses of powerful drugs . . . have produced much evil." Confusion reigned; a mass of uneducated, fanatical patent-right holders developed—united only in their belief in a botanical system of medication. A local doctor had two favorite prescriptions: "One he called 'Tincture Botanae,' which he gave when he did not know what else to do, for it is emetic, sedative, cathartic, tonic, and expectorant, and cannot fail to hit somewhere.' The other he called 'Diabolical Pills.'"

With common sense and caution Dr. Still steered a middle course between the harsh measures of the "regulars" belonging to the State Medical Society and the unorthodox remedies of the "irregulars." He did not believe in chemical drugs (particularly mercury); he disapproved of surgery, water-cures, and electric shock. His treatment might be best classified as humanitarian with a concern for the comfort of the patient—an attitude ignored by many physicians of the time. So his reputation for cures spread and his practice prospered. He built an office and residence at Cross-Roads and became the third largest real-estate owner in Medford Township.

After Dr. Still died in 1885, people forgot about his book which had been privately printed in 1877. His memory was still revered in the backwoods, but pineland folk were not readers. At the death of Dr. Still's daughter in 1930, a Medford resident and collector, Frank Wolf, found the well worn auto-biography in the family home which was about to be torn down. Henry Beck reported the incident in a Camden newspaper; the story of "The Doctor of the Pines" was reprinted in *Forgotten Towns of Southern New Jersey,* and the collectors' search for copies of the autobiography was on.

Dr. Edward C. Jennings, who lives in the Benjamin Wilkins' house, owns the copy found in 1930. Between the yellowed pages was a handwritten bill dated 1852 so it is likely this was Dr. Still's personal copy. Dr. Jennings, a member of the Medford Historical Society, kindly lent the volume for this facsimile edition.

Despite reports to the contrary, Dr. Still's office remains on Church Road just east of the Mount Holly Road (Route 541); a historical marker is on the site of the residence, which was demolished. The Still property is now owned by Dr. Robert J. Trollinger of Medford. North on Route 541 are the homes of Thomas Wilkins and Amos Wilkins, the farmer James Still was "bound to for a term of three years." (p. 30) The Wilkins's graves can be seen in Friends' burial grounds in Medford. Dr. Still lies in Colemantown Cemetery, Mount

Laurel, where a monument was erected some time after his death.

Another Medford resident often referred to in the book is "Dr. B." (*See* pp. 91-94, 111, 143, 177.) Since the time of his practice in the town coincides with Dr. Still's, he is probably the Andrews Eckard Budd whose biography appears in Woodward and Hageman's *History of Burlington and Mercer Counties:* "After attending two full courses of lectures at the University of Pennsylvania, he graduated in the spring of 1842. . . . He began the practice of medicine in Vincentown, Burlington Co., and remained there about two years and eight months. From thence he removed to Medford (same county) and followed his profession eighteen years." Dr. Budd's home still stands on North Main Street, Medford.

Modern readers of Dr. Still's life may well be more interested in his philosophy than in his medical theories. His comments on race relations are still relevant. In the Camden *Courier-Post* (May 20, 1971) Stephen O'Keefe wrote a feature article titled: "Doctor of Pines' Philosophy Could Heal Today's Racial Ills." Dr. Still complained often of prejudice, but he stated: "It has long been my opinion that the colored people as a race have much to blame in themselves for their present condition." (p. 228) So he looked at both sides of the problem. He also wrote: "I have been opposed to colored schools wholly because they were against the principles of Christian fellowship. I think that co-education would be beneficial to each race." (p. 239) Perhaps James Still's honorary title should have been Doctor of Philosophy rather than Medical Doctor.

Thanks are due the following members of the Medford Historical Society who helped make this book possible: Clyde W. LeVan, for the idea of a facsimile edition: Dr. Edward C. Jennings, for permission to use his valuable copy of the autobiography and reproduce the handwritten bill; Everett F. Mickle, for the photograph of Dr. Still's residence in 1876 from the *Burlington County Atlas;* George Fleming, for lending his copy for indexing and reproducing the title page; Harold Leach, for design and manufacturing.

Margery Cridland
Medford Historical Society

James Still

EARLY RECOLLECTIONS

AND

LIFE OF DR. JAMES STILL.

PRINTED FOR THE AUTHOR BY

J. B. LIPPINCOTT & CO.

1877.

INTRODUCTION.

I PROPOSE to give a concise sketch of my early recollections, well knowing my inability to write history or launch into the depths of the learned.

It was my lot in early life to be debarred from the advantages of education. It is very true my parents were poor and unable to school their children, as was also the case with many others in our section of country. Their main object was to provide bread for their children, and they had reason to congratulate themselves on their success were they thus fortunate.

It so happened that I received three months' instruction in reading, writing, and arithmetic, which completed me to start out in life. If so be I should prefer a professional life of any kind, as doctor, lawyer, or minister, or whatever pursuit I chose to follow, I stood robed with three months' education with which to start. For this much I feel truly thankful, when I look around and see so many deprived of even this.

I know the critic will find fault, and also laugh; but I ask him to put himself in my forlorn condition, and perhaps his sympathy would be excited for those less favored than himself. Let the case be as it may, I feel contented to let it pass before the public for what it is worth. Perhaps I might have done better, but my time has been very limited while engaged in the work. I have written mostly at night, being busy through the day attending to office duties.

Being frequently called upon a dozen or twenty times a day, I could not collect my thoughts for any length of time. Indeed, my whole life has been such that I did everything in a hurry. I hope my advantages will not be viewed collaterally with the learned and great men who have had access to seminaries, where the mantle of some functionary or dignitary has fallen upon them. Bright advantages have never been my portion. It cannot be said of me that I sat at the feet of the learned or drank from the fountains from whence all knowledge flows.

I hope this book may be a stimulus to some poor, dejected fellow-man, who, almost hopelessly, sits down and folds his arms and says, " I know nothing, and can do nothing." Let me say to you, Study nature and its laws, the source from which these mighty truths are drawn. Great minds are not made in schools. I am speaking to men whose pecuniary circumstances are such as to prevent them from being partakers of these blissful privileges.

A great mind is planted within us in the beginning of our lives, and, like other plants, it needs cultivation and watering from the best fountains. If these are out of reach, cultivate and water as best you can, and trust to the great Ruler of the universe for a crop, and you will not be disappointed in reaping a bountiful harvest, though you are often caused to feel depressed for want of a proper mode of utterance when in the company of the learned. Nevertheless, they will understand you if you cannot understand them.

It might be presumed by many that I am opposed to an education. Such is not the case; I only think it strange that educated men, who have been so fortunate, should treat their more unfortunate fellows with such contempt because they do not possess their abilities in the same refined manner. When we view mankind, we see the great fall into error as well as the small. When we look at art, we find that great and learned men are not foremost at all times. When we look at our greatest inventions, they are the production of unlearned and poor men with great brains.

Whilst going through the United States Mint a short time ago, "There," said my conductor, "is the handsomest engine in the world; built by a man who never served an hour's apprenticeship at any trade." It is not all who serve apprenticeships, even under the best skilled workmen, that come to be proficient mechanics.

You will observe that a number of young men —say a dozen—study law, and only one or two of the number become popular lawyers, although all receive their diplomas, and that is all they can boast of. What can be the matter with such? They are lacking of genius, I believe. All persons are born with certain gifts, which sooner or later develop in them, and I think those gifts should be cultivated, let them be of what sort they may, so that they lead to honorable pursuits. Covet no man's occupation because he prospers in it. Thousands on that account fail and fall. The only road to wealth and happiness is perseverance and frugality.

In very early life my mind was much troubled about what should be my occupation in life, although I had almost daily presentiments, from three and a half years of age until I was twenty-two or three, that I should be a doctor. At times I would be discouraged, seeing no way to obtain a knowledge of such an important profession. I supposed I would need to go to college, and there be instructed, but I had no finance to enable me, and, worst of all, I was not of the right color to enter where such knowledge was dispensed; therefore I saw nothing but thick clouds and darkness before me. I relied, however, on that great Hand which made the sun, moon, and stars. I believed that He could work when none could hinder.

Finally the day came and the clouds were driven away, the sun shone brightly, and my way was lit up, and I entered in with marvellous success. Although I had the batteries of the learned to contend with, and the infantry of the prejudiced to face, yet I succeeded admirably in quelling the foe. Their war implements were what their

fathers had used, and were old and rusty. Although they were frightful to those unacquainted
with the field of action, yet one with the bright
sword of truth would chase a thousand, and two
would put ten thousand to flight; or should you
meet them singly in the field, they are clad with
their best armor, swelling and foaming like bold
Jordan, whose streams at times are perfectly terrific.
They prance and foam like maddened steeds; they
pride themselves as Goliaths; they challenge to
the battle with the intent to destroy; but should
there come one to meet the champion only with
his sling charged with a smooth stone, *nature*,
from the brook of truth and justice, he slays the
mighty giant, and wins the battle.

The stupid minions of the giant will exclaim, It
was only a boy with a stone, not made for war; it
was only by chance this mighty feat was done.
Then they carry their champion from the field and
bury him in an oblivious grave, and return to their
homes, proclaiming, A mighty champion is slain
by accident; and with boldness they endeavor to
perpetuate his memory.

I also propose to give a concise synopsis of my
practice of medicine, and what I know about dis-

eases generally. Specially fevers, which are a great terror, although, when judiciously treated, I consider them more easily controlled in the early stage than any other class of disease. I am confident that I am not in command of language sufficient to demonstrate these truths in their proper light, yet I will make the attempt, hoping allowance will be made for my lack of education. I will endeavor to delineate what kind of medicines I think best or safest to use in practice for the benefit of suffering humanity.

CONTENTS.

EARLY RECOLLECTIONS

AND

LIFE OF DR. JAMES STILL.

CHAPTER I.

I WAS born in Washington Township (now Shamong), Burlington County, State of New Jersey, April ninth, one thousand eight hundred and twelve, at what was called the Indian Mill, then owned by one Samuel Reeve. My father's name was Levin Still, and my mother's name was Charity. They were born in Maryland, and were slaves. My father bought his freedom, and then undertook to free his wife by bringing her to New Jersey. They came into the State a few years previous to my birth, and settled finally at the

Indian Mill, where my father followed sawing to sustain himself and his family.

They lived at the mill one year, during which time I was born. My mother has said I was born with two teeth, which seemed mysterious, and many supposed it a foreboding of ill to me. She thought I could not be born with teeth and live to become a man, the occurrence was one so uncommon.

My father with his family moved to a place about one mile off, called the Thompson place, and there spent one year. From there he moved in with an old colored man by the name of Cato, hoping to better his own condition and that of his family. At the Cato place I date my first recollections, being about two years and six months old. I recollect my father bringing me a pair of new shoes from Lumberton. In trying them on they did not prove a fit, so he took them back to change them, at which I cried sadly. At this place I also recollect first seeing a constable. His name was Israel Small. He was riding on horseback in pursuit of some one of the Milligan family, who lived opposite to us, and so impressed was I by the terror of the law, that I did not know at that time but that in the constable was vested all power on the earth. The earth was very small to me then, and so was I very small, but as time passed on my thoughts grew larger.

At this place I recollect the birth of my brother, John Nelson, I being two years and nine months old. There were several women about on that day, and all appeared happy and gay. I have not forgotten the nice tea on the occasion, of which, when I think, the taste is fresh in my mind. I remember, too, that some one of the women brought the baby to me, and asked me who it was, and I could not tell. They told me it was my little brother, and tried to make me pronounce the words; on which I said, "little bludder," and they laughed at me. An old lady, by the name of Rhoda Barnes, seemed to be the chief among them.

I well remember, too, the house where all this occurred. It was an old log house, one story high and an attic, with one door, large fireplace; no glass windows. I think there were two rooms on the first floor and one on the second. People were poor in those days, and had no stoves to heat their houses, nor carpets on the floors. Women

wore short gowns and petticoats. Six or seven
yards would make a gown to be worn on First
Day, as it was called.

As time glided on, everything began to look
cheerful to me. It so happened that Dr. Fort was
called to our house to vaccinate the children, my
brother John being about six months old at the
time. The doctor performed the duty, and I have
sometimes thought that the virus being inserted in
my arm must have taken better than usual, for the
sting of the lancet yet remains. From that moment I was inspired with a desire to be a doctor.
It took deep root in me, so deep that all the
drought of poverty or lack of education could not
destroy the desire. From that day I did not want
any knowledge save that of the healing art. It
grew with my growth and strengthened with my
strength. My thinking faculties were aroused, and
I soon commenced to practise. Among the children I procured a piece of glass, and made virus
of spittle; I also procured a thin piece of pine
bark, which I substituted for a lancet. Thus was
the little acorn, which was intended to become an
oak, thrown into the thicket, not knowing that it
should ever again be seen or heard from, but there

was One, unseen, who cared for and watered and protected it.

After living with Cato one or two years, my father bought some land of him, and built a house on it. It was a log house, with one door and no glass windows in it. He moved into it, and we then were a happy family with a home of our own. Land was cheap, being from one to three dollars an acre in that part of the country. My father being a very industrious man and naturally of a high temper, everything he undertook he thought ought to yield to him. He had a large family by this time, and for their well-doing he labored assiduously. Finding the task too great, some of the children had to be put out in other homes. As the girls were the eldest, their turn came first. I, at that time, was only a consumer and not a producer, so it became my turn to stay at home, and delight myself in playing about the yard and looking forward to the time when I should be, like Dr. Fort, riding around healing the sick and doing great miracles. These thoughts would come over me with an enrapturing sense. Strange to say, I never delighted in toys or playthings or childish sports. Time passed on, and I came to be eight or nine years old, when I was put to work at chopping wood and getting rails in the cedar swamp and making charcoal. In the summer we picked huckleberries, and in the autumn cranberries.

In those days we saw hard times,—frequently short of food and clothing. Often we would not see meat for weeks. I remember, at a time in which we had gotten some meat, I was eating at the table, and each one had his share given him. I was saving mine until the last of the meal, when Jacko, an old black cat, took it out of my hand and put it in his mouth. I sprang at him, caught him by the throat with one hand and took the meat out of his mouth with the other, and placed it in my own mouth. So much saved by activity. This poverty at times would cloud my vision when I looked forward to my most cherished hopes.

I was about eight or nine years old when I first was sent to school, and this was a new era to me. I soon became acquainted with all of the children, but their sports were not pleasure to me. At most of the plays I was a poor hand. I learned none of them, not even so much as a game of marbles, and at ball I was only chosen to make up the number.

We went to school only in bad weather, and worked during the fair weather. There was one thing I soon learned, and that was to curse and to swear, although this was never known to my parents. Our school-books were the New Testament and Comly's Spelling-Book, in which we learned everything that was useful for man to know. The teacher taught us grammar in those books, and taught us how to pronounce everything improperly, and we knew no better. I am glad that in these days a better order of things is instituted in our own State, and that the merit of a teacher is known before being employed.

My mother was a stanch Methodist, but my father was not, although a great reader of the Scriptures and a believer in them. I often thought his whole soul was wrapped in the twenty-fourth verse of the thirteenth chapter of Proverbs, which reads, " He that spareth his rod hateth his son ; but he that loveth him chastiseth him betimes." I had no particular love for that passage of Scripture.

Our nearest neighbors were an Indian family, the name of whose head was Job Moore. His

eldest son was named Job, and he and I were very
social. We played together, and fished and hunted
when opportunity would admit. My father was
very strict with his children; we were not allowed
to run about to play on Sundays like the other children. All of us that could read must stay about
home and read the Scriptures, and those that could
not read must study their spelling-lesson. Believe
me, Sunday was a long day. At intervals we were
allowed to leave the house, but obliged to stay
within calling distance, for fear father would love
us according to Scripture.

When I was about ten years of age, father
bought a yoke of oxen, and it became my lot to
drive them with him. Of this new business I was
very proud at first, but it soon became a source of
great vexation. We used to cart wood to Medford, and the oxen were so slow it appeared to me
that I should die of tire. Our condition, though,
was changed for the better, for we used to carry
our provision on our backs, but now we could cart
it on the wagon. In all this, the sting of Dr.
Fort's lancet never left me. Oh, how many have
lived and died without knowing anything of the
rugged road the poor of the world have to travel!

Often half starved for food, half naked, barefooted, with no one to look up to but a poor, dejected father, who feels the same sting.

I remember one time, before we got the oxen, we were out of bread and meat, and almost everything like food, and father left home in the afternoon to go in the country to get something for his family. He stayed all night, and returned the next morning with flour and meat on his shoulder. Mother made a cake, fried some meat, and put up some for brother Samuel and myself to take for dinner, as we were going cranberrying. We had not got out of sight of the house before we turned into the woods and ate it, and then fasted for the rest of the day. I remember an incident while I was driving the oxen. My father sent me to Ballinger's Mills one day with a grist. It was about four miles from home, and it was a very cold day. When I reached there my feet were so cold that all feeling was gone. I pulled off my shoes and held my feet to the fire to warm them, and before I knew it or felt it I had burned all the soles from my stockings. Josephus Smith was miller at the time, and saw it.

Our house, at this time, was surrounded by

forest, and only now and then a habitation near. Wild deer were plenty, and many persons took great pleasure in hunting them for sport and for food. Bears also inhabited the neighborhood. I remember when three of them passed through my father's field, not more than one hundred yards from the house, and walked about under an oak-tree in search of acorns, and their tracks were visible the next morning. The fox, the raccoon, and grouse were also inhabitants of our wild forest, all of which have now given place to the husbandman. The Indians, who used to be seen in scores travelling through the wood, and the marks of whose axes were left on many a white oak, trying its qualities for basket stuff, are all gone, some to their last resting-place, and others to foreign climes, to be heard from no more forever.

I must have been now about eleven years old, and our prospect for living grew as we boys grew more able to work. Finally, my older brother, Samuel, was put out to live with Aaron Engle, and that was a soul-trying day to me. The day my brother left I was eleven years, eleven months, and twelve days old, and parting with him almost broke my heart. As he was the oldest, I always had something to lean upon, but now all was gone.

I made one solemn resolve at that time that I never would curse again, which resolve I never but once violated. Keeping my promise solaced me at times. At this period I commenced to read the Scripture, and all the religious tracts I could get, during all my leisure moments, day and night. I read by pine-light, as we had an open fireplace, and candles were not plenty. I neither learned songs nor dancing. Mirth of all kinds was unpleasant to me. I had a great love for truthfulness, and was very fearful of the devil and ghosts, particularly at night. I was also afraid of Indian Job. He was a tall man, I think six feet and six inches high. He would often get drunk, and go whooping about in Indian fashion, which was a great terror to me. Job was killed finally. A wagon containing a cord and a quarter of green oak wood passed over him in one of his drunken frolics. I was at first elated at this, but afterwards came to consider that a dead man or a ghost would be more difficult to evade than a living one. The matter so disturbed me that at night I scarcely dare stir from the house for fear of seeing him. I only quieted myself by thinking that if he did appear I would call upon the Lord to deliver me, although I sometimes doubted if He would do this, so great a sinner did I feel myself to be.

I recollect one night that his son Job and myself went to meeting, and as we were standing outside of the door we heard a shrill shout, which seemed to come from the graveyard where old Job was buried. Young Job said to me, " That's daddy." The young man's experience, together with my own fears, was like a thousand daggers driven to my heart, and great horror seized me. I trembled in every muscle and sweat from every pore. We went into the meeting-house, and I watched the door and windows, expecting to see old Job enter, but he did not come. In the walk home I feared we would meet him, and, as the reader may imagine, I should find myself in that case no better off.

My father sent me to the same school-house where the meeting had been held at another time —in the evening—to get the master's spectacles. I had to obey him, not daring to say no, lest he would manifest his love to me in the Scriptural fashion I before spoke of, so I went along with my heart rising in my throat. When I came to the door I stopped to listen for a moment, to see if all was right. Hearing nothing, I made a rush at the door with the key in my hand, unlocked it, pushed it open, flew to the desk, seized the spectacles, ran out of the house, and started for home. When I reached the edge of the hill, where an old house had once been standing, but now in ruins, I saw a broken brick and a cent sticking up from the ground. I grabbed the cent, and ran for life, and when fairly out of danger thought I had been re-paid for my trouble. I mention these things that my younger readers may see that untrained imag-ination will lead one from the right way.

CHAPTER II.

I PASS, next, to give our progress in life. As good Providence would have it, we were doing pretty well. My father traded his oxen for a horse, and then we boys thought we were doing nicely, although we had to work as hard as before. We chopped a great many cords of wood for different persons; we also lived much better and were clothed better. I was now growing to be in my fourteenth year, and my father hired me out to Israel Small for one month, to help them in digging potatoes and husking corn. While there I learned to play dominoes. They were the first I had ever seen. The whole family played, and I played with them. I never played again after leaving there.

I was very determined in everything I undertook, and I always knew where to find a thing that belonged to me if it had been disturbed by no one else. My knife, or other things, I never lost, as most boys did. As I advanced in years the horizon of my life widened, my vision expanded, and things began to look more beautiful. The thought of Dr. Fort's lancet would run through my mind and set me to musing, Can it be that I will ever become a doctor? If so, how will I obtain information or to whom shall I go? Then I would think, I know no black doctors, and white ones will not instruct me, and I have not the means to defray my expenses at college. As I chopped wood, thus would I muse, wishing the time to roll around when I should be a man.

It went very slowly to me, and I could not hurry it, so, as I thought, I would commit my life to Nature's God, hoping all things that ended well would be well. I formed a habit of doing anything at the time appointed for it to be done. If I promised to do a thing, I did it. If I had to go anywhere, I was always on time. There was nothing like present time to me, and if I commenced to do a thing I would finish it. I never ate except when hungry, and then, if in a hurry or busy, would scarcely take time for that.

I began to think and wonder why the black race was so despised by the white race. I won-

dered if the same Great God made both races, and
why there was so much distinction. I would look
at the cattle and all the beasts of the field, and see
them all colors; yet there was more unity among
these than among people, even of the highest profession. I would look in the forest; there were
the pine, the oak, the cedar, growing in harmony
together, fulfilling the duty designed by the Creator, no complaining, but each, in its own way, beau-
tifying the earth. Then, thought I, professors are
not Christians except in name, for the same rule is
practised in the church as out of it: all that are not
white must sit on back seats, no matter how long
they have been Christians. Then I would think
of heaven, with all its glorious inhabitants, and
wonder if any were shut out from there on account
of color. The twenty-sixth verse of the seven-
teenth chapter of Acts cleared my thoughts on this
subject, for there I read, "*God hath made of one blood
all nations of men for to dwell on all the face of the
earth, and hath determined the times before appointed,
and the bounds of their habitation.*" This and the
verses after satisfied me that all had a chance for
heaven, that merit alone was the qualification for
admittance into that kingdom of everlasting rest.

I used to think that all boys had more knowledge than I. They sang songs and danced, and knew how to play games, and talked of places and towns, all of which I could not do, so I would keep silent in their company. As to dancing, I thought I would learn it if ever I should get time; but it so happened I never found time, and I do not think that I ever shall now. Novels I never read, because I could see no real truth in them.

My father took my brother Nelson and me to Philadelphia with him. There were no steamboats at that time on the river, and we crossed on horse-boats, went up into the city, and into the market. I never saw so much provision; there appeared to be enough for the whole world. We went up Chestnut Street, and there seemed to be all the magnificence in the world. Thought I, When I get home I will tell the boys what I have seen in Philadelphia. I did, and they laughed at me and said they had been there many times. This disturbed me very much, and made me retreat into my silence again. I suppose I was about sixteen years old at this time, and I think it was that same fall that my father hired me to Aaron Engle for one month. My brother Samuel was living there,

and to me the reunion with him was a very pleasant one. Not so much so to him, however, for he
was five years older than I and had chosen other
company. I stayed there the month out, and
then went home, and remained at home until the
fifth of February, eighteen hundred and thirty.

On that memorable morning we boys went, as
usual, to the woods, and when my father came
where we were at work he found fault with my
laboring with my coat on. There was a very
heavy sleet that morning, which was the cause of
my doing so, but I dare not say anything in reply,
lest he should love me again according to Scripture. I began to be pretty tired of his mode of
loving, and I determined to leave him, let the consequences be what they might. He did not stay
long in the woods, and soon after he left I also
left, and went to Amos Wilkins's. He would not
hire me, but said he would see my father shortly.
Accordingly he saw him, and I was bound to
Wilkins for a term of three years and two months
and five days. My father was to receive one hundred dollars for it, and I was to have three months'
schooling,—one month each winter. At the expiration of the term I was to receive ten dollars

and a suit of new clothes. I was very sorry to leave my mother, as I knew she had hard times in her daily life. I used to think of her, also of my younger brothers chopping in the woods and I not with them. It was comfort to know that He who cared for the birds and all other creatures would care for my mother in her troubles and trials.

I had great faith in Providence and in prayer, and prayed for my mother and brothers while at Wilkins's. During the first year we had our drams every morning, and I soon became a lover of strong drink, and needed to increase the dose to get the effect. In harvest time all used spirits, and it was plenty in the field and in the house. I soon found that I was liking it too well. One Sunday morning I rose early to get my dram. I had it in the glass ; I added molasses to it, and went to the pump, pumped water into it, and turned it into the pump-trough, and walked into the house, with a firm resolve to drink no more, which resolution I have never broken, not even on Wilkins's premises at the time, although plenty of liquor was made there, for he owned a distillery.

Every fall now my duty was farming instead of wood-chopping, as formerly. I liked the farming

best.   I also had more time for contemplation,
being often alone ploughing in the field or carting
from the woods.   How many times have I seen
visions of my future course open to me!   At times
I was entirely absorbed by these visions, and it
would appear to me that I was practising medicine
with great success.   I could see my patients coming from all parts of the country,—the lame on
beds, consumptives almost gone.   So great seemed
the number that I had not time to attend to all.
All kind of diseases imploring my help ; many
seemed given over by skilful physicians, yet I
treated them with success, to the astonishment of
all who beheld.   I seemed in my visions, too, to be
riding over the country healing the sick.   Some
sang my praise, others derided me.   I often could
not tell whether the visions were fancy or prophecy.
Of this I leave the reader to judge.

At these times I would frequently be in ecsta-
sies, not able to tell when I came to the field,
or how long I had been there, until the horn
aroused me by summoning to dinner.   I would
sometimes blame myself for these mental states,
and resolve never to give way to them again, but I
was not able to control them, and would only re-

solve, to find myself launched again on the ocean of my imagination without rudder or compass or any one to guide. I had hope only as an anchor and a faith in Him who rules all things, believing He would bring my frail bark to its desired haven. Time passed slowly, a month seemed long as a year. I dared not open my lips to any one lest I should be laughed at. Well, thought I, the day will come when I shall be a man, and I will earn money enough to go where I can study medicine, for I supposed there was no other way to obtain it. When winter of the first year came on at Wilkins's and I was to have my month of promised school-ing, I felt very delicate about entering the school, as I could not write, or even cipher in addition, although I was now in my nineteenth year. What to do I could not tell. I feared the smiles of those who were younger and knew more.

I was to begin on Monday morning, and on Sunday previous I went to my brother Samuel, who lived a short distance off, and asked him to show me how to perform addition. He readily complied, got the book, and commenced, suppos-ing it would be an easy task, but he had con-siderable difficulty to make me understand about carrying one for every ten. At length it dawned upon my mind. I was delighted, and on Monday morning went to school. I think Nathan Prickett was the teacher. I met many strange faces and some scoffs. I applied myself so assiduously that in a few days I was attacked with a fearful pain in my head, at first only lasting an hour or so, but so severe that I was almost frantic. Every day it increased, until it was only broken at short intervals. I survived it, however, and finished my month at school, and was set to carting out of the pines, and to ploughing in the early spring.

The pain in my head continued, and caused me great suffering; no one, when I spoke of it in the family, seemed to notice me. I procured some bayberry bark from the root, dried it on the stove, and, making snuff, snuffed it into my head, and from that found no relief. Finally, in carting from the wood one day from a place called Christopher's Mills, I was suffering very much. I came to a little stream of water that crossed the road. I stopped the team and stood on the bridge for a moment, contemplating covering my head in the stream, and fearing at the same time it would prove fatal. If it does, however, I thought, I will soon be found by some one in the public road; so concluded to try the experiment. I took off my hat, and, setting it down, plunged my head into the stream about half-way to the ears. I got up, shook my head, and stood on the bridge again to await the result of my experiment. In ten minutes' time I was delighted to know my pain was gone and I was cured. Passing the same stream in a few hours afterwards, I again buried my head in the water up to the shoulders, and for twelve years I was not troubled with headache.

My summer passed very well. I had nothing to annoy me but work, and that I feared but little, for I could do my part in the field among the men. I had no books, no money or friends, no one with whom to keep company. I went about but little on Sundays or at night. My second year at Wilkins's did not differ from the first. The visions troubled me about as before, and my inclination grew stronger to be free. I spent my second winter at school under a teacher named John Fowler, and improved some in the knowledge of arithmetic, and also in penmanship. When my month expired I went back to the plough and all other duties allotted to me, and fulfilled them without murmuring.

I often thought myself the most desolate person in the State,—no one with whom to commune of my future hopes. The world was growing larger to me with all its mountains of difficulty, whose peaks seemed to tower to the heavens and appear insurmountable. I have thought many times since that had I known " Nobody's Song," I should have sung it every day; but I have learned it since I climbed the mountain-tops, and will give it a place among my recollections, hoping it will cheer somebody when cast down.

NOBODY'S SONG.

I am thinking just now of nobody,
    And all that nobody's done,
For I've a passion for nobody,
    That nobody else would own.
I bear the name of nobody,
    For from nobody I sprung,
And I sing the praise of nobody,
    As nobody mine has done.

In life's young morning, nobody
    To me was tender and dear,
And my cradle was rocked by nobody,
    And nobody was ever near.

I was petted and praised by nobody,
   And nobody brought me up,
And when I was hungry, nobody
   Gave me to drink or sup.

I went to school to nobody,
   And nobody taught me to read,
I played in the streets with nobody,
   And nobody ever gave heed.
I recounted my tale to nobody,
   For nobody was willing to hear,
And my heart it clung to nobody,
   And nobody shed a tear.

And when I grew older, nobody
   Gave me a helping turn,
And by the good aid of nobody
   I began my living to earn.
And hence I courted nobody,
   And said nobody's I'd be,
And I asked to marry nobody,
   And nobody married me.

Thus I trudged along with nobody,
   And nobody cheers my life,
And I have a love for nobody
   Which nobody has for his wife.
So here's a health to nobody,
   For nobody's now in town,
And I've a passion for nobody,
   That nobody else would own.

CHAPTER III.

My third winter came for me to go to school, and as it was my last chance for education, I must improve it and prepare for graduation. I went to Brace Roads school, with Sandeth Frazier as teacher. There was a young girl in the school at whom I must needs look a little, which possibly retarded my progress, nevertheless I made pretty good time.

After I had been in school some two weeks, Wilkins and a hired man were carting, and let the horses run away. I thought the accident occurred through carelessness, and on expressing this to Wilkins he insisted on my stopping a week to drive the team. I at first refused, but on his insisting was obliged to yield. I commenced with great care, and all went well until Saturday afternoon, when I was returning home with a load of pine boards. As I was nearing Cross-Roads the horses took fright at the clapping of the boards together over a rough piece of road. I caught them as they started to run, but we soon became entangled in the fence. With this, they knocked me down, ran over me, and got away from me. I supposed I was killed, therefore I made no attempt to get up. Daniel Bates came to me at last, and said, " Jim, are you hurt?" I did not know what to answer him, supposing I was badly hurt. I had no feeling ; but, as I did not die, I rose up and sat at the side of the road, awaiting my fate. Everything around me turned green, and the earth appeared to be reeling so swiftly that I had to cling to it as best I could. The horses ran about one hundred and fifty yards, and several men ran out and caught them. Although feeling pretty sick, I walked up to them, got on the wagon, and Samuel Sharp helped me to drive them home. Wilkins tauntingly asked me how I came to let them get away. I felt too vexed to give him an answer, and thought it none of his business.

I returned to school on Monday to pursue my studies as best I could, but I was very lame from my hurt for two or three weeks. I finished my month, and graduated of course, and left for the plough, the team, and whatever was allotted me.

The time was drawing near for me to choose for myself, and what to do or where to go I could not settle in my mind. I was like the aspen-tree trembling in every wind, well knowing my inability, but resolved that, " sink or swim, live or die, survive or perish," I would make an effort, trusting in Him who cares for the ravens, which have neither store-houses nor barns. Finally, that long-looked-for day arrived, the ninth of April, eighteen hundred and thirty-three. I arose in the morning and commenced to collect what little belonged to me, which, I assure my reader, I had little trouble in doing; two twelve-and-a-half-cent cotton handkerchiefs were sufficient to hold my worldly goods, and I was not long in performing the task of packing, the children looking sorrowfully on the while. The dark cloud of dread hung heavily over me as I bade adieu to the family and farm in Fostertown. After distributing some pamphlets and little books among the children, and receiving my freedom money from Wilkins, I took my all, one handkerchief on each arm, with the nine dollars and fifty cents I had just received, in my pocket, and started.

Where, or among whom I should land, I could not tell. I called at my brother Samuel's, who was then living near the Cross-Roads, to bid him and family farewell. It was a sore trial to me, but I performed the duty as best I could, with tears in my eyes.

Leaving Samuel's, I started for Philadelphia. I went by by-roads and through woods. After travelling about two hundred yards in a woods, I spied a large black-snake lying a little to my left. I seized a stick close at hand, and, killing the snake, threw away the stick and was about to gather up my pack and go on, when, on the other side of the way, I beheld another as large as the first. I picked up the stick again and killed it, also. Now, thought I, good luck will attend me, as I had heard say, " Kill the first snake you see in the new year and you shall kill your enemies." Hoping the old saying might prove true, I gathered my pack and started for the city. While thus travelling my thoughts were many, but I ever congratulated myself on killing the snakes at the commencement of my journey.

Again and again I deplored my poverty, thinking that, with not more than ten dollars' worth of clothing, and nine dollars and fifty cents in money, and without home or friends, my condition was a sad one. Indeed, I suspected that I might be taken for a runaway; but as I had my indentures, I thought that to show them would be sufficient proof of my honesty. I travelled along on foot and alone, with no one to molest, and at length reached Philadelphia. In the afternoon of the same day I went to my sister, Keturah Wilmer's, and stayed there during the night.

I arose in the morning, ate my breakfast, and after asking some questions and answering others in regard to the city and my expectations in life, I walked out to take a survey of the place. I went into Fourth Street, and was looking around at people and things, when a gentleman approached me and asked me if I wanted to hire. I said I did. He asked me where I was from. I answered, New Jersey. He then inquired how much I wanted per month, and as beginning was a new business, I did not know what to say. I asked him what employment I would need to follow, and he replied, work in a glue factory. This, also, was new to me; but finding that he offered me ten dollars per month and board, which was better than I could do in the country, I accepted his offer, and promised to come to his place in the morning.

"Where shall I find your place?" I asked. As he answered me I thought certainly good luck is in waiting for me, although the wages being so good at the first offer, made me a little dubious of the man. He told me that his name was Charles Cummings. We then parted. I went back to my sister's in Apple Street, and told her of my success.

She encouraged me to think it a good opening, and that I would do well at it. Gleamings of my future came over me that night, and I slept restlessly. Morning came, and I went to the factory. On entering the yard I thought I had come to the wrong place, for the stench was horrible. Having never been used to such smell or business, I was not a little chagrined to think that I was in a filthy fix, nevertheless was determined to keep my engagement and try the work. Mr. Cummings bade me good-morning. I returned the compliment. Then he showed me the cutting-room, and told me I must lay the green glue on the drying harrows. I began slowly, that I might gain some insight into the mode of handling.   When all hands were fairly starting, I caught the motion and thought I must begin.   I broke the first cake, but the second I carried to the harrow safe and whole.   I became an expert quickly, and was looked upon by the rest of the workmen as an old hand from another factory. The men had previously agreed not to instruct any new hands who should be employed in the business.   I soon became acquainted with all of them (there were about twenty), and found them social and cordial.   I was the only colored person in the factory.   So happily and prosperously and hopefully did the days pass to me that it seemed as though genial winds were blowing the clouds of despair from my path.

I had not worked one month out before my employer came to me and said he would give me twelve dollars for the first month, and wished me to stay on with him.   I agreed to do so, and when the month was up he paid me and said he would give me fourteen dollars for the coming month.   I was quite elated with my good fortune, was very saving, and deposited my money in the Savings-Fund as fast as I got it.   I began to think I will soon get money enough to go and study medicine. After working two or three months for fourteen dollars per month, which was Mr. Cummings's own offer, I thought I would ask for an addition to it myself. When I mentioned the matter to him he asked me how much I wanted; I replied, fifteen dollars, and he promptly gave it.

I soon was intrusted with all the care of the business in his absence. In his house we lived at fountain-head, better far than I had been used to. I kept no company, went to no places of amusement, drank no liquors. I concluded, finally, that I would buy some clothes. I went to a second-hand store and bought a frock-coat and vest and pants, so that I could go to meeting on Sundays. I soon had seventy-five dollars in the Savings-Fund, and a suit that cost about five or six dollars. When I had been at my work about six months I began to want to go to the country and see the old friends. I went to a clothing-store and bought a new suit that cost fourteen dollars, and then determined to go home to see my parents. On Saturday I started, took the stage at Camden, went to Medford, and then walked to Fostertown and found some old acquaintance. During the time I had been living on fresh fare in

Philadelphia I had been wanting some pork and potatoes. I was like the dog in the good book; I wanted to return to my former way of living.

I called at a place where I expected to get my supper; they seemed glad to see me and invited me to stay. I thanked them and remained, supper being ready. When seated, I looked at the table and wished myself back at Cummings's. It seemed the roughest table I had ever seen. There were clay-cold potatoes and pork, which looked as though it had been cooked a week, and no tea or coffee. I began to think that it was not pork and potatoes that I wanted. I took a seat, did the best I could, got up from the table not quite so well satisfied as when I sat down.

The next morning I started for my mother's, having always believed her the best cook that ever lived. The mothers of most children are the same in that respect. I reached my father's early in the day, in time to tell my mother I would like to have a good country dinner. She accordingly prepared it, and I enjoyed it very much. I was very glad to see her, and asked about the times and how she had been getting along; what troubles and difficulties came; whether her old age was more smooth than formerly, and how my younger brothers were. There were four at home at that time, and when we all got together it was a joyful meeting. We talked of everything we could think of, old and new. I could tell them I had money in the Savings-Bank, and that my prospects were bright. I intended to stay one week in the country, but after three or four days began to get restless, and concluded to return to the city. I bade my mother and brothers good-by, gave my mother a little money, and left my blessing with all. My father had gone early to Medford that morning, and was not home when I left.

I met him on the road about two miles from his house, on top of what we called the high hill, and whilst standing and talking with him, a large rattlesnake came out of the woods. I took a slab from my father's wagon, and despatched the snake. This was the first large live rattlesnake that I had ever seen. My visit home occurred about the fifth of September, eighteen hundred and thirty-three. I left my father and travelled on, stopping a day or so at my brother Samuel's, at Cross-Roads, and reached Medford in time for a morning stage, reaching Philadelphia at noon. All of the factory hands, together with Cummings's family, were glad to see me, and greeted me with shaking of hands. They asked me of my visit, what pleasure I had had, what I had seen and what reception I met with, whether warm or cold, and wished they had been with me to share my enjoyment.

I resumed my work in the factory, holding the highest position of any of the hands. In fact, I became a kind of arbitrator among them; if any dispute arose I was called on to determine between the parties, and generally with good success. We got along nicely in the factory, and all seemed to enjoy life, with its many blessings. Mr. Cummings was, naturally, a very energetic man, looked well to his own interest, and endeavored to make the best of everything. He would frequently use profane language to the hands, which was very unpleasant to me, and I told him there was no use in using it, and I hoped that he would not use it to me; "for," said I, "when I don't suit you, say so, and settle with me, and I will leave." He answered, "All is right between you and me, but some of the hands vex me so badly, I can't help it."

CHAPTER IV.

TOGETHER with glue-making, Mr. Cummings carried on bone-boiling, cowskin-whip making, manufactured curled hair for stuffing sofas and coaches and mattresses, and many other things; also neat's-foot oil for lubricating purposes. Altogether, the business was very lucrative. The glue was made from the trimmings from the tanners, and from sinews cut from beeves' feet, which needed to go through a process of liming before they were fit for glue. After being cut from the feet, they were boiled till very tender, then the liquid was drawn off through sieves into long troughs, called coolers, and was set aside until it became cool and stiff, resembling soap. It was then cut across with a knife about eight inches, and laid on a table to be cut into thin cakes with a machine made of brass wire. Then it was laid on nets, and the cakes had to be turned on the nets every day, till nearly dry. They were then taken off and strung on

49

twine, using a needle for that purpose. These strings were hung in the air, or under sheds, until fully dried for market.

Neat's-foot oil was made from beeves' feet by boiling. After removing the hoof, which was sold to comb-makers, from the foot, we removed the sinew with a sharp knife—the sinew to be used for glue after being limed in a vat for about two weeks. The feet were boiled till done, and then the oil skimmed off. It was barrelled for market. The round bone of the foot was sold to turners to make embellishments for umbrellas and other things. The flat bones were sold to button-makers, and the refuse from the boiling was thrown out for the hogs and dogs to feed on. Of dogs there were twenty, and hogs, many more. The dogs were kept for killing rats, which were very numerous. The factory stood over a little stream, so that the water could be raised at will. During times of heavy rain, the gates were shut down, and the water rising under the factory would drive out the rats, when the dogs, and all hands with them, would make war upon the pests, and kill two or three hundred in an hour. The smell arising from so much putrefaction made by boiling was very

offensive to persons not accustomed to it. Being
fairly initiated, one, however, would know but little
difference. I had previously been very delicate as
to smell and taste, but the factory completely cured
me.

Time passed on and brought us into the fall.
Business was very brisk, and I began to learn that
they could not make glue in the winter, although
other branches of the business could go on. I
began to contemplate my future course if I should
leave my present position. I made up my mind
that I should go to the country. As the cold winter weather came on business became more slack,
and I saw that Mr. Cummings grew more independent. I was ready at any moment to change,
and one day he came into the yard, and seemed to
be in an ill humor. He spoke rashly, and, as I
knew no cause for censure, I told him so. I said,
however, that I would leave if he would settle with
me. He demurred at this, so I stopped work,
went to an alderman, and brought Mr. Cummings
to a settlement. Having received my pay, I made
ready for the country with a little more to pack
than when I left it for the city. I had bought a
trunk, and was quite independent, packed in it my

goods, bade adieu to all hands, and set out in the stage for the place of my nativity.

I arrived at Cross-Roads some time in the evening, stopped at my brother Samuel's, boarded a few days with him, and then purchased an axe; got some chopping to do for C. Shreves, built me a cabin in the woods, about three miles from Medford, and lodged in it that winter. I chopped wood, did my own cooking, and stayed many lonely nights by myself. Sometimes I would have company, as there were several other young men chopping in the same place. They frequently derided me for being so saving, as I went pretty ragged. They gave me the name of Mr. Buzzard, and would often ask me when I meant to fly. I enjoyed the joke, and retorted by saying, "I shall some time be flying high in the pleasant air and looking sorrowfully down upon you, because you shall be wing-tipped and can't rise from the earth. I expect to shed my coat for a better, and you shall shed yours for a worse." I have lived to see my prediction fulfilled. I also said to them, "There shall come a day when you shall call me the eagle; then I shall not retaliate upon you." When I look upon the past, I think how little we know of the future. Few consider for what they live. They must have their good things first, and the worst last.

In the spring of eighteen hundred and thirty-four I left the wood, with some clear cash made by chopping. In the first year of my freedom I had saved over one hundred dollars. During this spring I hired with Josiah Thorn, on a farm in Fostertown, for about eight or nine dollars per month. I remained the summer and fall with him, and in the winter went to the woods again, chopped all winter, and cleared some money.

CHAPTER V.

In the spring of eighteen hundred and thirty-five, I again hired with Thorn. He had then moved on a farm near Ellisburg. There I conceived the idea of marrying. A young girl lived at Thorn's by the name of Angelina Willow.

I felt too poor to get married yet, as I had spent two winters in the woods, and had a little money and no prospect to study medicine. I finally determined that, with her consent, we should enter into the conjugal state. We talked the matter over several times. I had made up my mind long before this never to marry, but the more I talked to her, and the more I thought of it, the more strongly I became conscious of the meshes of love environing me. I then learned four love-songs, and sung them every day, first one and then the other,—sang them until I got married, and have not sung them since. The names of two I still remember, the others are long ago forgotten. " Barbara Allen" and " James Bird" are the two which have not escaped me. The resolution never to marry I concluded to call a mistake, as it had been made when very young, and although I had many doubts about my ability to support a wife, and thoughts of the future of which I had dreamed harassed me, I could see no good reason why Angelina and I should not cast our lots together, and on the twenty-fifth day of July, eighteen hundred and thirty-five, we were married.

We left Thorn's a short time after. She went home to her parents, and I hired with Thomas Eyre, near Lumberton, for one month. When the month was over I rented a room of Charlotte Ecabee, an old colored woman living at Fostertown. With fifty or seventy-five dollars we furnished our apartment, and commenced housekeeping. This was my third winter after being free, and the first since then that I had stayed in a house. I worked by the day, dug marl, threshed for the farmers, and chopped wood near home. I did pretty well, but cleared no money. On the sixth of January of this winter, eighteen hundred and thirty-six, it began to snow, and continued for two or three days. It drifted and blocked up the highway, so that travel was carried on across the fields. It impeded all out-door work for five weeks, in consequence of which there was not much for laboring men to do.

Many were driven to extremity, but I was independent, having something laid up beforehand. I did not want to draw upon my funds, however, and managed not to do it, for I was anxious to get me a home, as all prospect of studying medicine was gone. Many cares and expenses, also, that I had not foreseen, were coming upon me. Winter at last gave way to spring, and prospects were brightening. The lady of whom I rented the room gave up the house to the landlord, William Hammell. I then rented all of it from him for thirty-six dollars per year. I was to work for him when he wanted me. I got along as best I could, and worked for him when he had work for me, and at other times for Nathan Wilkins, the brother of my old boss, who proved to be the best friend I ever had, although I paid him for all he ever did for me. We had a little daughter born to us while we lived in Hammell's house, and we called her name Beulah, after her grandmother. I made up my mind to spend my money in buying a home, if I could find one, and only having one hundred dollars left, I knew it would not go far towards it.

As I knew Amos Wilkins to be a moneyed man, I went to him and asked him if I should buy a home for three hundred dollars, would he lend me two hundred to help pay for it. I suppose he thought that he would never get the money again, so he gave me no encouragement. I felt friendless and alone. I continued to inquire about little houses and lots for sale. I could hear of none. One day I went to Cross-Roads to see if I could hear of a house that might be bought on low terms. Whilst there some one told me of a lot of brush land, just back of the Cross-Roads, owned by Isaac Haines. I concluded to see him, and did so. I asked him if he owned such a lot, to which he replied that he did. I asked him what he would take for it, he answered one hundred dollars. " Is that the lowest?" I asked. He said it was. " Well, when will you make me the deed?" " In a day or two." " Very well," said I; " I will give you the money." So we parted.

In a day or two he handed me the deed. I

paid him ninety dollars, and gave him my note for ten. It so happened the bargain was closed before the neighbors knew anything of it. When it was known that I had bought, all the prejudices against my race leaped forth. Execrations were heaped upon me, because the prospect of a colored neighbor was not acceptable to them. For the first time I learned the reason that I had not been able to buy a home just before this, where I had offered one of the citizens of Cross-Roads his price for a one-acre lot. When I came to realize that his reason for refusing was because he wanted no colored person near him, all my indignation was aroused. I felt also that my life had many prejudices and influences to combat, and that I had nothing to depend upon but my own energy.

Well, thought I, I have a lot, but neither house, nor money, nor friends. In this dilemma I went to Nathan Wilkins, told him what I had done, and asked him if he would help me to get a house on my lot. He discouragingly talked the matter over, and then said that he had a house in the pines which he had commenced to build and never finished, and that he would sell it to me for fifty dollars.

Having accepted the offer, I was considerably exercised over the matter of moving the unfinished house upon my own lot. I got Levi Jones with his four-horse team, and two or three other two-horse teams, with about one dozen men, who all gave me their work except Jones. He charged me four dollars. I had a basket of victuals prepared. We all set out in the morning for the pines. Having reached the place, we laid the house in four parts, loaded it on the wagons, and, returning to Cross-Roads, placed it upon the small lot I had purchased. It was very small, only twelve feet by twenty. It needed to be raised and put in order to live in, and how this was to be done I scarcely knew. As to friends, I had none· My money was gone. I was sensitive to refusal, so asked no one to lend me. I had nothing but myself to rely upon. I employed Amos Waterman to raise the house and to fix it so that we could live in it. There was no mason work except putting up the chimney. On the fifteenth day of March, eighteen hundred and thirty-seven, we moved into it from Hammell's house at Fostertown.

Anna and I were much pleased with our new

home. The house was surrounded by small pines and thick brush. I needed to clear a place for a garden, and as it was spring went to work. I dug a hole on the lower part of a little elevated piece of ground near the house, and there we got water. There were two rooms below, and two rooms above, in the house: a parlor and kitchen on the first floor, and a spare-room on the second to accommodate our friends when they came to see us.

The land was to be cleared, fencing to be obtained, a living to be provided, and duties pressing with new claims into my life that altogether seemed nearly insurmountable. I had been used to adversity and poverty, and I made up my mind that it would not do to go back, for dark as any future may seem there is some semblance of hope that will play about it.

I cut pine poles to make a garden fence so that I could raise some vegetables, and found daily work to sustain my family. I got bricks and brick-paved my house, doing the work myself at leisure times. Thus I managed to save all I could. Some portions of the house I had plastered by the coming winter. In eighteen hundred and thirty-seven I dug marl, chopped wood, and threshed, and whatever else I could get to do. All seemed to be going well until spring, when my wife was taken with a heavy cold, which terminated in consumption. We did all we could to restore her, but without avail.

During this spring Ira Haines sold me four acres of land adjoining mine. All of my land was now brush land, and not enclosed. I was obliged to give Nathan Wilkins a mortgage on all. I worked out in the daytime, and grubbed at night, taking poles and brush to make fencing. There were in all six acres of land. I got two or three acres ready for the plough, had it broken up, sowed in buckwheat, and the summer proved to be a very dry one. Not rain enough to lay the dust fell at any time for the space of five months. Vegetation perished, and the grasshoppers were very destructive ; consequently my buckwheat perished with the rest.

My wife continued to grow more feeble, and the indications were that she was not long to be with us. It was a sorrowful time to me. I felt that I must soon be left alone, my friend and my all was to be taken from me. My little daughter,

Beulah, and myself would need to solace ourselves as best we could.

I had one great consolation, and this was that Angelina made her peace with God. She died in the faith, on Sunday, August twelfth, eighteen hundred and thirty-eight. Whilst dying she exhorted all around her to meet her in heaven, where she should soon be with angels praising God, where was neither sickness nor sorrow. She bade me and our little girl farewell, hoping to meet us in that heavenly land.

CHAPTER VI.

I FELT wholly undone when my wife was gone, with nothing in the world left me to dote upon but my little Beulah. I placed her at my mother's, and I am sure that my parents never had a child of their own whom they treated so tenderly.

What to do in this forlorn condition I did not know. I secluded myself from all company except such as I was compelled to be with. I walked the woods and roads alone, ate but little, and grieved bitterly. Finally I made up my mind to make a vendue. I sold the most of my goods, reserving a bed, a few chairs, table, and some other articles, which I left in my house. I then walked about, mourning for one who could not come to me, but to whom I could go. So I determined to strive to go to her. I prayed much. In all of my travails little Beulah seemed to be my comfort, and I went to my father's every week or two to see her. One

day, whilst on my way there, I was meditating
and praying fervently, when all at once the light
of life shone over me, and the Spirit of God filled
my soul.   I was transported with joy and peace
unspeakable.   I looked round, and it really seemed
to me as if the trees, the sky, and the atmosphere
were all singing praises.   I felt that heaven itself
had come down to me.   My heart was filled with
love to God and all his creatures.   I seemed to
have no trouble now, nor was it hard to be sub-
missive to the will of God for taking my wife to
Himself.   This experience happened to me on the
road to my father's, about one mile from Ballinger's Mills, in August, eighteen hundred and
thirty-eight.   When I reached my father's and saw
him and my mother, I thought I loved them better
than ever before, and my little girl looked like an
angel.   All that I could say was, " Happy day and
thrice happy deliverance !"   I returned home, and
when I went to bed it seemed as if I was lying in
the arms of Jesus, and when I awoke I was still
happy.

   This ecstasy lasted me about a week.   I tried
to get into my old state of mourning and praying
for the pardon of my sins, for which I felt quite

rejected. I could not see why there remained no power within me to mourn for my sins as formerly. So one day, when I had returned from prayer in the woods, where I had seemed to receive no blessing, I picked up my Testament, and opened it by chance to see if I could find something to console me. Opening at the eighth chapter of Romans, first verse, I read it without seeing anything in it to help me. I laid down the book and went out. I returned in a little time, opened it again, and found that the leaves parted at the same chapter. I read the same verse, closed the book again, and went out, not noticing or seeing particularly the hidden meaning of the verse as it applied to me.

I returned after a short time, and opened the book once more, when, behold, the same chapter and verse presented themselves to me as before! It impressed me strangely that I should open the book the third time at the same place, and thought I should pay it more attention. I commenced at the verse which I had each time previously read, " There is therefore now no condemnation to them which are in Christ Jesus." I threw the book down, and did rejoice in God my Saviour from that moment. I dare not ever after doubt the sensible manifestation of the Spirit of God.

I have passed the spot on the road where I received the new birth many times since, and I never have neglected to offer up my supplication to God for his bounteous goodness. I then joined the church. Previous to this I had had fears of thunderstorms, but all fears were dispelled in my new trust in the Lord Jesus. I stayed at my house alone, lay me down at night, and slept in peace, with no fears to harass me.

Again the desire to study medicine came over me, but there appeared no way to accomplish it. I kept bachelor's hall most of the time, or until late in the fall, when I let an old lady, by the name of Delilah Johnson, move in with me, and also Charles Lopeman. We succeeded very well together until spring. During this time I had no notion of ever getting married again, and I expected to spend the rest of my days a widower. I worked out for Nathan Wilkins and Moses Livezey, and, as the days passed and I grew more and more lonely, I began to think about finding me a wife.

There were many difficulties attending single life. I considered that it would be better for me to have some one to tell my troubles to; so, finally, went to see Henrietta Thomas, a young girl living with Robert Woolston, at Vincenttown, and opened my mind to her on the all-important subject of marriage. She being, like myself, with no home, none but the kitchen of some one else, was not long in making up her mind, and on August eighth, eighteen hundred and thirty-nine, we were married. On August eleventh of the same year our little Beulah died, one year after her mother. Each died on Sunday.

My new wife and I went to housekeeping, and battled the world as best we could. One thing we had in abundance, and that was poverty. As I had known what it was to be in want, it was no stranger to me. We set out to provide a living. By being saving and industrious we were not negligent to add to our comfort. Our little place was to clear up and to fence, which would require time, labor, and money. I worked out, to make a living, grubbed and cleared at odd times and at night. I bought a cow at length, and then we had to build a barn. I managed to get material, and had a small barn built by Elwood Waterman. At this time things began to look more prosperous in

many ways. I was raising something on my
ground to eat, which now I had enclosed with a
brush fence.

On July twelfth, eighteen hundred and forty,
little Jimmie was born to us. We continued to
struggle on, and, although poor, were full of hope.
For myself, I was a great believer in Providence,
ever believing His care to be over all; therefore
I always had an eye single to Him in all things,
knowing that my course was just and honest in
my dealings with men. I always trusted in Him
to deliver me from my enemies, and I truly believe
He did, for it seemed to me as if most of the neighbors were endeavoring to vex me in some way.

The man who kept the tavern near me seemed
to delight in annoying me in any way that he
could. Poor soul! he knew no better, and Providence, in His own good time, removed him.

Death again visited our family. Brother Joseph
was called away from time to eternity, September
ninth, eighteen hundred and forty-one. He, too,
made a happy end, which fact gave us less cause
to mourn for him, although he passed from us in the
bloom of youth.

As I lived back of Cross-Roads and not very near

a public road, I used to wish that I could buy the land out even with the road; but the time had not yet come, and I had to content myself without it. On December twenty-fourth, eighteen hundred and forty-two, death revisited us, by taking away our father. He was sick only a short time, sent for brother Samuel and me to come and see him, and when we came to him he wanted one of us to go for Isaac Glover to write his will, who came and did it. I then sent to Philadelphia for my sisters to come home and see him. They came immediately, arriving late in the night. Knocking at the door, father arose from his bed and let them in. Sister Mary said she felt annoyed that she had come so far to find him no worse, and she was greatly surprised that he should be walking about. Brother William went home still later. I think that father told him where to put his horse and what to give him. Perhaps all went to bed, but death was there and served his summons before the morning, and father was no more.

He provided in his will that mother should have all of his estate after paying what debts there were, and at her death the personal property was to be sold and divided among five of his children, and

Samuel was to have the farm. I was to have a seven-acre lot of brush land during my life, which, after that, was to pass to my son James. Samuel and I were left executors, and after a reasonable time we made a sale of such goods and effects as mother did not want. I bought the horse at the sale. When we came to settle up and pay the debts, there was nothing left for the five children named in the will.

I took my horse home, and concluded to go at something better than work by the day. So I bought a still of Wm. Jones, near Mount Holly, and got him to instruct me in the business. I took it home, and set it myself, and began to distil sassafras roots, and, in the summer time, herbs of various kinds. I went to town every two weeks with oil, and felt much pleased with my prospects. While I digged the roots my wife tended the fire for me, so that all went on well. This was in the year eighteen hundred and forty-three. The practice of medicine, on which I had set my heart earlier, would occasionally come into my mind, but I thought the day was past and my fate sealed. I continued with my business that season alone. I also learned to make the essence of peppermint and many other kinds of essences. I then thought I was getting on finely. I dealt with Charles and William Ellis, druggists in Philadelphia. In often being there and seeing medicine, my old anxiety for the knowledge revived, but how to bring about the matter I did not know.

CHAPTER VII.

ONE day I went to the city, and George King
went with me. I sold my oil, and we were to
meet at an appointed place for breakfast. When
we met he asked me where I was going, to which
I replied, "You can go where you like, I am
crazy." He laughed. The idea had just struck
me to get a medical botany to instruct me in the
knowledge of plants. I went up Chestnut Street,
to where I have never known since, and saw a
large book-store on the corner. Entering, I asked
the man behind the counter if he had a medical
botany. He looked at me and answered in the
negative. There was an old gentleman in the
store, who noticed me, and said, "Has thee a
notion of studying medical botany?" I answered, "Yes." "Then," said he, "thee must never
give it up." The old gentleman was dressed in
Quaker garb, and said to the storekeeper, "Can't
thee tell him where to get one?" The man hesi-

tated a moment, and said, " Perhaps you can get one on the corner of Eighth or Ninth Street, at a book-stand."

The Quaker-looking gentleman seemed to be quite interested, and asked me my name and where I lived, and told me I could get one somewhere, and that I must not give it up. His way and manner startled me, and I wondered to myself if he saw anything in me that I was keeping secret. He bade me farewell, hoping I would be successful. I left, and have never seen the store or the man since.

I went to Market Street, to a book-stand, and asked the young man for the book I was in search of. He handed me one, and when I inquired the price he answered, " One dollar and twenty-five cents." I offered him one dollar, which he refused, and while looking over it I found it was a floral work; so I told him I would not take it. He became somewhat enraged, and said he would compel me to take it, at which I left him and the book, not knowing where to go next. I wandered off, and found myself up Fourth Street, above Arch. There I saw a kind of an herb-store, with a few books in the window, and the sign

DOCTOR THOMAS COOK. I went in and asked him if he had a medical botany.

He looked at me as though he knew my mind, and handed down the book. I asked him the price; he replied, "One dollar." I handed him the money, took the book, and was about to leave, when, showing me a volume, he said, "There's a book you ought to have." I asked him the price, and he answered, "One dollar and twenty-five cents." I told him I would call in about two weeks, and perhaps would take it.

After reaching home and reading botany for two weeks I grew more anxious, and at the end of two weeks found myself again at Dr. Cook's office: took his dollar and a quarter work, which contained formulas for preparing medicine, and some directions for its administration. One of the great mysteries that had so long perplexed me was now laid open. The second book I had obtained was one of only one hundred and sixty-four pages, giving instructions for making pills, powders, tinctures, salves, and liniments. I then thought I would need to study anatomy, which would require some time. Besides, I had no books, and no one to instruct me. So I thought that I would use the books in my possession to the best benefit, and possibly in the course of a few years the way would open for further study, for I thought that I knew nothing about diseases. I had never been among the sick, and did not intend to do anything for anybody.

CHAPTER VIII.

I DID not know that the time had come for me to practise. I made up some tinctures for my own family, and one of the neighbors was known to it. One of the daughters of this neighbor developed scrofula, and he had me visit her. I gave her medicine which soon cured her. I thought it no great thing, for it always seemed to me that all diseases were curable, and I wondered why the doctors did not cure them. This case was Mary Anna Carson, daughter of Abraham Carson. The neighbors began to call upon me, and I administered to them with great satisfaction. As I was engaged with my distilling I did not find time to attend to medicine. One day, as I was coming along the road, I saw a hedge of sassafras growing by a fence. I went up to the house and asked the lady if Mr. Glover was at home. She replied that he was, but not feeling well was lying down. I told her I should like to see him. She went in, and he

presently came out. " Good-morning, Mr. Glover,"
I said. He returned the compliment, and then lay
down on the ground. I was in a hurry, and not
wishing to annoy him I said, quickly, " Mr. Glover,
I called to see if you would let me dig the sassafras roots along your fence ?" " If you will cure
me of the piles," he answered, " I will dig them up
and give them to you." " I do not want you to
dig them," I said, " but I will cure you if you will
let me have the roots." " Well," said he, " come
and get them."

I went home, borrowed a little wooden mortar
and one of those long stones or Indian pestles of
old Thomas Cline, with which to pound the herbs.
Having prepared the remedy, I took it to him,
and it had the desired effect. In a few days he
was well. I was pleased, and so was he. It did
not occur to me at this time, however, that I was
practising medicine. I thought that I was but
doing a friendly service to a fellow-being. People were beginning to call upon me so much that
it interfered with my business of distilling, so I
employed Abraham Carson to help me dig roots
and assist me in my work. I paid him one dollar
per day, and things seemed to be going pretty well

for a time, but I soon discovered that I was not doing so well as when the work was wholly done by myself. Still I continued to employ him during most of eighteen hundred and forty-four, and it then seemed best to me to continue by myself and to discharge him.

About the year eighteen hundred and forty-five my mother came to my house on a visit, and telling me about John Naylor's daughter, who was seriously afflicted with scrofula, and had been since she was one year old, I said to my mother to tell Mr. Naylor to bring his daughter down, to get a place for her to board near me, and I would cure her. After a little time he got board for her at Abraham Carson's. He told me that the doctors said she could not be cured, and that they had refused to do anything for her. She was, in reality, the most distressing case I had ever seen. Her neck and breast were ulcerated, and so swollen and sore that she could not raise her hands to her head. Her presence was offensive, and it was not pleasant to be in the room with her. In two weeks from the time I began treatment of her case the child could comb her hair, of which fact she was very proud. Whilst I was treating her I often called persons in to see her. To some she was too unpleasant to look at; others exclaimed, "Jim Still, if you can cure her you can do anything." And, again, others would say, "If the doctors cannot cure her how do you expect to do it?" I continued on, nothing doubting, and in about nine or ten weeks she was ready to go home, and nearly well.

I sought no custom from any source. I was obliged to keep up my business of distilling in order to make a living, and after a little time I saw that I could not afford to hire Carson, and undertook to do myself the distilling and the doctoring. My practice increased, and I had little time at the distillery; so I resolved to give it up, and to attend to the practice which seemed growing upon me.

I had no wagon to ride in, so I made one. The body was of rough pine-boards. The cover was of muslin, made by my wife, arranged over old hoops, which I had bought of Moses Livezey. She went to John Egbert's drug-store at Medford, and bought lead-colored paint, and painted the body of the wagon. The top was left white. I then was ready for my work. A cigar-box answered for a medicine-chest, and I filled some opodeldoc bottles, with large mouths, with such medicine as I wanted. My calls were many, and I rode continually. The cases under my care I cured. The most strange thing of all was that I had never seen diseases of any kind, yet they seemed plain and open to me. I never undertook a case without looking to Providence to guide me in it, and I truly think He did. The doctors laughed at me behind my back at seeing my white-top wagon and myself going through the country healing the sick, and I laughed myself sometimes, but I could do no better. Let them laugh who win, I thought, and he that loses may cry.

My greatest trouble at this time arose from the fact that my practice was paying nothing. I continued for some time, hoping to have something to pay my debts and furnish a living for my family. I often thought it strange that those to whom I was indebted were generous enough not to ask me for money. I lived very frugally ; when my wife found it necessary to buy a dress for herself she would take enough material from it to make a little dress for one of the children. Often we were quite needy ; also, I wanted books that I had seen at Dr. Cook's. One day I went to Philadelphia and called on my sister Mary. I asked her if she would lend me six dollars for two weeks, which she did.

I went to Dr. Cook's, got the book which contained the history and description of all diseases, and found its study a great help to me. It seemed as though the history of the diseases of the human frame was familiar, and as though study renewed the possession of a knowledge which I had had previously.

After practising for some time, I was told that I was finable for practising without license; neither could I collect pay. I went to a justice and inquired, who said I was not finable and could collect my pay. I employed this same man to post my books, for which he charged me ten dollars. I then got him to issue against some of them who were owing me, and they carrying it to a higher court I lost my suit. What to do at this I did not know. There were several hundred dollars on the books at the time, and I had a suspicion that the justice was working only to get me into a net or to get a fee now and then.

Thinking over the matter, I concluded to go to a lawyer and get his counsel. Accordingly, I went to John C. Ten Eyck, of Mount Holly, and stated my case. He took but little notice of me, as though he did not want to bother with me. I told him I would pay him. I asked him if I was fina-ble for practising without license. He said no, but told me I could not collect for medical services without license. " You can sell medicine," said he, " and charge for delivering, and then you can col-lect it just the same as for anything else. There is a fine for giving prescriptions, but you don't give them; you sell medicine and there is nothing to stop you." I came home, changed my way of doing, commenced to collect as I went, and soon began to recover my condition.

In the mean time, William Springer sent for me to come to his daughter, who had been afflicted with hip-disease for seven years. I attended her with good success, and he paid me manfully. This was a great help to me, and he and his family were well pleased to find the daughter cured.

From this time I began to gain financially, and also in practice. I was able to liquidate my debts, and it seemed as though the dark and cloudy morning of my life was about to give way to a bright and shining day. My property was still encumbered with Nathan Wilkins's mortgage, to the amount of one hundred and sixty dollars. I saw that I must have a new carriage to ride in. I bought a new rockaway wagon of Thomas Lee on time, and managed to pay when the time was up. I then left my white-top wagon at home, and was able to ride in one of more modern respectability.

I was desirous of getting a lot on the main road. I saw one of my neighbors who owned one, and asked him about it, but he could give me no answer. After some time, he said he would sell me two lots, which contained two acres, for the sum of one hundred and fifty dollars. " I will give it," I said. I had not money enough by me, so I went to Amos Wilkins to get him to lend me sixty dollars. He hesitated for a little time, and said he would let me have it if I would give him surety. I thought it hard, as he knew me so well, but I saw no way save to comply. It was the first time in my life it had been demanded of me, and I did not know upon whom to call. I went, however, to Thomas and Micajah Gardiner, and asked them. They endorsed the note for sixty days, but said they would do it for no other person, for they had been heavy losers by that business. Bates then gave me a deed, April twenty-fourth, eighteen hundred and forty-nine.

My next ambition was to have a house upon the lot near to the road. Money was still scarce, and the venture seemed a risk. I went to Charles Haines and contracted with him for building-stuff. John Wiley did the building, and Edward Stack-house came to help him. It was put up in the summer and fall of eighteen hundred and forty-nine. The house was thirty feet front and eighteen deep, and we were to move our old house to it for the back wing, and to serve as a kitchen. We moved into it on December twenty-seventh of the same year, and found our new home a comfortable one. At the time the house was raised the tavern-keeper adjoining made all the fun he could of my acts, and said that I ought to have a bunch of nigger bones to hang to the top of the rafters. How little did he think when making these expressions that it would not be long before God should call him to account, and his property pass into the hands of the man whom he delighted to revile!

CHAPTER IX.

I was getting along now quite satisfactorily. I was paying off my debts, and my practice was increasing. Every two weeks I went to Jackson Glass-works, to Waterford, to Pumpbranch, to Tansborough. This occupied a day. Most of my practice paid me as I visited, by which means I was able to get considerable money; and I was thus enabled, too, to lift myself from the dark cloud of financial depression. About this time I conceived the idea of buying the tavern property should it ever be offered for sale, and remarked to this effect to some of my neighbors. In the mean time my friend, Nathan Wilkins, died, which disturbed me somewhat, knowing he held a mortgage on my property. I began to make preparation to be called upon by his executors should they see fit to do so. John Nixon also died. I had been hoping that Nathan Wilkins's son, Benjamin, would assist me in buying the tavern, but on my speaking to him about it he said he could not, and that he wanted me to pay the mortgage his father held against me. "Well," said I, "I will do it;" but this seemed to destroy all prospect of my getting possession of the tavern property. The day for the sale came, however, and I had not much notion of going, for I had no money to buy with. I had said previously to my friends that I wanted it, and concluded at length to attend and watch the progress of the sale.

It was set up and no one bid. Going low, I thought; just the time to buy. Without the least hope of becoming its purchaser at that time, I made the first bid, fifteen hundred dollars. At this, I saw some of my neighbors determined that I should not have it. They commenced bidding, and ran it up to twenty-six hundred dollars. I well knew they could not buy, and I let them have things their own way. I went home to my office to attend a patient, and whilst there I was seized with neuralgia. I laid off my overcoat and said to my wife, "I guess I will not go back again." My pain growing better, I put on my coat, saying, "I will go back and see how they are getting on," though I supposed the sale to be over.

When I made my appearance, the crier said, "Come, doctor, we are waiting for you." "You need not do that," I replied; "why have you not sold it to some one of these gentlemen?" After deliberation, they concluded to set it up again at my first bid. I knew my financial condition to be low, and resolved not to be drawn into it unwarily.

A butcher from Haddonfield was one of the men who had come to purchase, but he made no bid. The Medford butcher came in, and, to keep the other out, bid at the property, and it was struck off to him. At this he seemed to be in a dilemma, for he could not comply with the conditions. He then came to me, and wanted me to take it off his hands, and said he would give me twenty-five pounds of beef if I would take it, but I declined. Afterward Mr. J. Oliphant and Mr. B. Shreve came to me and said if I would sign the conditions I should have it. They asked me how much I could pay on it, and I answered, "Not one dollar." Mr. Oliphant then said they must have fifty-five dollars, and if I would sign the conditions he would get that out of the bank, and added, "You can pay that in four months, which is the longest time the bank gives."

I signed the conditions, and gave my note for fifty-five dollars, supposing that Mr. Oliphant endorsed it, but when I came to take it up there was no name on it but mine. The place had been knocked off at nineteen hundred and seventy-five dollars.

I gave a mortgage on all my property, got the deed April twenty-fourth, eighteen hundred and fifty-two. Previous to this, March twenty-fourth, the same year, I had paid off the Nathan Wilkins mortgage. I now found myself much more in debt than before. I rented the tavern to Barzillai Prickett for one hundred and fifty dollars for one year. I had the house and sheds to repair, which cost me about five hundred dollars, all of which I managed pretty well. B. Shreve took a mortgage on my property for fourteen hundred and seventy dollars, which I paid off in about three or four years, leaving one still held by Elizabeth Braddock, of five hundred, which she did not want.

I made up my mind that we would soon need

to have a new house, and began to make preparations for it, when by chance I found that the Thomas Cline property was to be sold. I delayed building, and bought this property in eighteen hundred and fifty-four, of Brewer Hultz, for five hundred and five dollars. I borrowed the money of Amos Wilkins, and gave a mortgage, which was never recorded.

I could not help at this point looking back to whence I started first, in the woods back of Cross-Roads, when I could get a front lot of no one; and now a front of nearly half a mile, extending along the road, was mine.

CHAPTER X.

In September, eighteen hundred and fifty-five, I made a trip to Canada West for recreation. I was gone from home about three weeks. It was not a very pleasant trip, owing to personal difficulties. Canada is a fine country, rich lands, and very large timber,—much larger than I had ever seen in the States,—such as white-oak, hickory, walnut, and many other kinds of wood. The people seemed as happy under the rule of the British lion as under that of the American eagle; indeed, I thought the colored people much happier.

I was sitting in my office one evening after my visit, thinking that as I had been away I would not have much to do for a time, when a man came in, introduced himself, and asked if I was the doctor. I replied that I was, upon which he said that he had a very sick daughter, and wanted me to go and see her. I asked him how long she had been sick, and he answered, "Eight weeks."

"Who is attending her?" I asked. "Doctor B., of Medford, and also Doctor T., of Moorestown." "What is the matter with her?" "Typhus fever, the doctor says." "Well," said I, "I shan't go." "Why?" "Because you have two doctors, and I don't intend to interfere." "I will go and see Doctor B. to-night, and discharge him; then will you go?" I said, "Perhaps I will." "Well," said he, "I will come to see you again to-night, or in the morning, and let you know. She is not at home, nor can we get her there, but is at Cross-Keys, at S. T.'s. The doctors have blistered her all the time on the legs, and she must die without some change."

In the morning, about seven o'clock, he returned and said, "I saw Dr. B. and discharged him." "Very well," I replied. "What time will you be there?" he asked, "for I want to be present when you are." I harnessed the horse, and away I went, reaching the house a little before him. I knocked at the door, and Mrs. T. came. The moment I saw her I felt vexed because I had consented to go, for the cold looks she gave me were enough to have subdued a lion had she met him in the forest. I had seen the like before, however, and knew how to treat that kind of an affront, as well as a sick patient.

After a little, Mrs. T. asked me up-stairs to the sick-room, and there lay the patient, cold and clammy. I approached her and made every effort to induce her to talk, but all in vain. I talked to her mother to get what information I could. She said they could keep nothing on her stomach, even water was rejected. I thought to myself that I was in a tight place, yet, under Providence, I would do what I could for her.

I knew well that Dr. B. would rather hear of her death under my care than otherwise. I left her some medicine, and as I went I could see cold looks from some, while others looked encouragingly. I thought I understood her case; I could find no fever about her. I gave her medicine to calm her stomach which acted like a charm, and anything she took was retained. In two weeks they could move her home, where she soon got well, to the great delight of all her friends. As I thought of my experience in this case I could not help mentally exclaiming, Science is at fault, or ignorance (as the fraternity call my little knowledge) must be wisdom !

After my return from Canada, I built an office
eighteen feet front and forty feet back, one story
high, with basement of the same dimensions.
Three rooms were on the ground floor, and three
in the basement. Two of the basement rooms
were provided with fireplaces for boilers to make
syrups, and the front room in the basement was
intended for a cooling-room. Of the three above,
the first was for a drug and medicine department, the second or middle room for a recep-
tion-room for patients, and the back room for
keeping all or any crude medicine. This made
me a very convenient place for my business,
although the doctors and others laughed at it,
thinking I would soon run my practice, office, and
all into the ground. It endured the storms, however, pretty well, and I had no fault to find or
reason to complain.

I had by this time gotten able to procure
drawers and bottles, and also mortars and pill-
machines, and almost everything necessary to fit
up my office. I had, too, a nice medicine-chest to
take with me when I went out to see patients, all
of which I began to feel proud of. I had a good
horse, too. Sometimes Dr. B. would call me

" Black Jim," by way of derision, but I was careful to attend to my own business, and not others'. I was too much engaged with my own interests to attend to what was said of me. I believed that merit was superior to birth, or even to the color of a man's skin, and I am satisfied that nature taught me the truest philosophy.

In eighteen hundred and fifty-nine I commenced to rebuild the tavern. I had the old part torn down except a little at one end that was good, and built a new part forty feet front, and thirty feet deep, and three stories high, and completed it the same year. I then rented it for two hundred dollars per year, after taking to myself seven acres of the land.

The next year after building I found myself ready to pay all of my debts. I was still owing Amos Wilkins the five hundred and five dollars that I had borrowed from him, and he called at my place one day in the fall and asked me if I could lend him fifty or seventy-five dollars. He said he was trying to make up some money for Hammitt, and could not collect any. I told him that I could, or was able to let him have two or three hundred if he wanted it; for, said I, " I

intend to pay off all of my debts in the spring."
" You do ?" said he. " Yes, I do ; you can have
all your money now, if you want it." He went
home, and the next morning he came back and
said, " If it suits you, I will take the whole, and
give you up the mortgage." " Very well," said I.
I went to his house, paid off the mortgage, and
returned home a happy man. I still owed Elizabeth Braddock five hundred dollars, which I paid
in the following spring, March twenty-third,
eighteen hundred and sixty-one. I then owed no
man anything, and of this fact there was one
proud man in Jersey.

My practice was still increasing, my wife and
children able to go better dressed, table a little
better supplied, and friends growing more plenty.
I recollect that when I told Amos Wilkins that I
intended to pay off all of my debts in the spring,
he exclaimed, " You do !" with astonishment, and
when I answered yes, he said, " By blood ! I never
expected you would ever pay them." I felt a little
chagrined, but said nothing. I saw then why he
had refused me money without security. His refusal did me no harm, however, for it made me
more frugal in all of my habits, and helped to fix

the determination within me to succeed in whatever I undertook. I now found that I was making
a little more money than I wanted to spend, so
that I could lend some now and then to a good
man, or one in whom I had confidence. This was
a great and gratifying change to me.

Indeed, I would look back to see whence I
started, what a rough road I had to travel all alone,
and the many difficulties and dangers through
which I had passed. I thought of the tavern-
keeper, too, who in his lifetime would deride me
and represent me falsely to my patients, although
I think he saw, before he departed, that I had been
a help to him in bringing custom to his house,
actually putting bread into his mouth. But we all
err and make mistakes in life, and of my memory
of him, as of many other unpleasant things, 'tis
best to " let the dead past bury its dead."

I had but little to fear now, as I saw that the
lions' mouths were closed, and some of the more
grim of them chained by the chain of truth whose
links were forged by the hand of the Great Arti-
ficer who laid the foundation of the earth and
stretched out the heavens as a tent to dwell in.
Yes, by Him who calmed the raging of the sea,

and said to its proud waves, " Thus far thou shalt go and no farther," and Him will I ever reverence sublimely!

There was very little to combat with now but my practice, and it seemed to me that all of the worst cases called upon me to attend them, and, as a rule, I treated them with surprisingly good success.

I recollect attending a young lady who had been sick for seven years. She had been visited by several different physicians, who had all abandoned her as incurable. I was sent for finally, and I found her pale and very much emaciated, skin dry and shrivelled, loss of appetite with prostration, feeble pulse, and almost without hope. I talked to her, and thought at the same time that she was not a desirable patient. I left her some medicine and went home, thinking that if she should die under my treatment there would be great rejoicing, and there were those who would hold me accountable for her life.

I went to see her two or three times, fearing I had undertaken too much, and as I could see but very little, if any, amendment, I concluded to treat her case the best I could, and leave the event to

Providence. I gave her what I thought would reach her disease, and it acted like a charm, and I was well pleased with it. In the course of a few days I called, and as I drew near to the house I discovered several wagons standing before the door. I drove up and found the house nearly filled with men and women, all looking sad and gloomy.

As I entered I saw the mother pacing the room, with handkerchief to her eyes, whilst she uttered sobs of grief for her supposed dying daughter. I drew to the bedside of Mary and said, " Miss Sooy, how are you this morning ?" She shook her head without uttering a word. The mother exclaimed, " Poor Mary is dying !" Then fell on me the weight of censure. What could I do or say to console a grieving family ? Something must be done. I took Mary by the hand, felt her pulse, looked her steadfastly in the eyes, and said, " Miss Sooy, you are not dying, and will not die this time. I know that you and every one must die sometime, but you will not die now ; and you must take these bitters and I will come to see you again."

At these words I could see a change in her countenance as though to say, You know more about it than all the rest. This was a gleam of hope to me. I left for home and felt very much troubled that day and night. The next morning I drove over to see her, fearing the consequence, and dreading to approach the house lest I should learn the sad intelligence that Mary was gone. When I entered, I watched narrowly the countenance of every one I met, and read in them that Mary was still alive. I was a little elated, pushed my way to the sick-room, glanced at the bed, and there was Mary yet on this side of the grave. I approached her with, " Good-morning, Miss Mary. You are better, I see. Did I not tell you so yesterday?" She smiled, and her mother, drawing near, smilingly said, " Mary is better; she seemed to change last night." I said to her, " If I had not happened to have come yesterday, you would, in all probability, have lost your daughter; but now she is better, and I think will get well."

Mary continued to improve, and finally fully recovered her health, and afterward married. For the providential restoration of the daughter, the family poured upon me copious showers of blessings never by me to be forgotten. I believed then and still believe that Mary would have died had I not persisted that her time was not then come.

CHAPTER XI.

ANOTHER case than that in the preceding chapter now presents itself to my mind: that of an old lady who had been afflicted between fifteen and twenty years, and who had been treated by several doctors without benefit, some of whom pronounced her disease dyspepsia, others liver-complaint or consumption. She had vainly tried, beside, the virtue of many patent medicines. Her symptoms were loss of appetite, costiveness, dry skin, pain in the stomach, retching of an acid fluid. She had strictly confined herself to a diet of unbolted wheat-bread, without coffee or meat. There were times when it seemed to her that death was preferable to life. As I had known her some years before I commenced to practise, I would not say anything to her about her affliction, except to ask her, when I met her, how she was. I often thought of her, however, and wanted to help her; but I was opposed to humbug, and had a shrinking delicacy from soliciting any one to try my remedies, even when I felt a confidence in their being benefited.

One day I was sitting in my office, and Mr. W. came in. I was pleased to see him, supposing he had come after me to go and see his wife, but he sat down and talked for about two hours, when all at once, in a hurried manner, he said he must go home. As he rose, he added, " My wife, Margaretta, wanted me to come after you and ask you to come and see her. I do not know that it is any use; but you must come." " Very well," said I, " I will come to-morrow morning, about ten o'clock." He then left for home, and I was pleased to think that I had an opportunity offered to cure or to administer to one so long afflicted. The next morning I prepared my box, and off I started full of hope. I arrived at the house at the time appointed, saw Mrs. W., and commenced an examination. I asked her how long she had suffered and what she had eaten. She told me exactly as she could the period of her suffering, and that she had eaten nothing but Graham bread, without coffee or tea.

" Do you have sick stomach?" " Yes, three or four times a day." " Do you vomit?" " Yes,

nothing but hot, sour water." "Do you per-
spire?" "No, I have not been in a perspiration
for ten or a dozen years." "Do you have any
pain?" "Yes, violent pain in the stomach before
vomiting, and then I am obliged to lie down."
"How do you rest at night?" "Very poorly."
"Well, Mrs. W., I think I will make you sweat
before I leave. I am going to give you some
medicine, and stay to see how it operates." I
made all necessary preparation, and then gave her
a dose and said to her, "Mrs. W., I think if this
operates rightly it will make you sick; have a
wash-bowl ready."

Within thirty minutes, with the perspiration
issuing from every pore, she began to vomit, and
what was ejected was in appearance like the kell
of a calf partly decayed, thick and viscous, with
offensive smell. I remained with her several
hours, or until the stomach became calm, and left
her strengthening bitters, with a promise to return
in a few days, which I did, and found her, as I
wished, free from pain and vomiting, and with a
general moisture of the whole surface.

In a few weeks she was well, and able to eat a
general diet, with comfortable nights and refresh-

ing sleep. I suppose this subject to have been far past sixty years of age at the time. She lived a number of years after her recovery, and enjoyed good health. She remarked to me when she had become well, " For two weeks after you commenced treating me I felt so strange that I thought you had killed me, but I never meant that you should be ungenerously judged had such been the case."

Was not this enough to make one who had not been blessed with the advantages of an education feel proud and grateful that he could be a benefactor to his race ? Oh, to whom should I be thankful but to the great physical Teacher, who teaches as never man taught ? Yes, 'tis He whom I shall adore, and whose Name I shall praise forevermore. We see that nature teaches the truest philosophy. God has made nothing in vain, and His eye is over all His works. He careth for the sparrow as for the eagle, and all His ways are truth and justice.

Another of these strange cases was that of a man living near Mount Holly, who was very sick, and had been for some time. He was attended by all the popular doctors of the place, both allopathic and homœopathic, until he, finding their skill was not prevailing in his case, concluded to send for me. His wife and her brother came for me one Sunday, and stated the case, and wished me to go and see her husband.

I refused on the grounds that other physicians were attending him, and that I would not intrude. They went home, and I heard nothing more about him until the next Sunday, when the brother came, saying that his brother was still ill, and never could be any better under his present treatment. I objected for a while, but he strongly insisted. I consented and went. Found him very sick, prostrated from long illness. I examined him, and administered medicine which proved of the utmost benefit. He soon recovered his natural health, to the great delight of his family and friends, although it was quite humiliating to the pride of the profession.

CHAPTER XII.

I THINK it will not be out of place to give a concise history of my mother in my early recollections. She came to live with me during the last years of her life, and I felt much consolation in administering to the comfort of her declining years. Well I knew that her past life had been attended with many cares and trials. She was born a slave, and in slavery reared to womanhood. Four children were born to her in her time of servitude, two sons and two daughters. Her anxious spirit longed for freedom, and no way presented itself but that of flight, and escape by flight she effected at a convenient season, leaving two little boys in bondage, and taking with her her two little daughters.

She fled to New Jersey, and took up her abode there. Often did she have cause to tremble for fear of her old taskmaster, well knowing that the law was against her, and that he had a right by the laws of her country to claim her and her children, and carry them back to slavery. There was no one to whom she could look for protection. She loved her children as other mothers did, but there was no heart to pity nor hand to save. In this disconsolate condition she looked to the Lord of glory and committed her all to Him. It was not long before He freely accepted her petition and rewarded her with an evidence of acceptance with Him. In this she rejoiced much until the day of her death.

She was frugal and industrious, a good wife and a good mother, always striving to train up her children in the fear of the Lord. Many and many a time when she has been singing her favorite hymns it has seemed to me as though she were enjoying some far-off happy company. I have heard her say that she found peace to her soul with God about six months before I was born, which would make it in point of time somewhere in the latter part of the year eighteen hundred and eleven. She was esteemed by all who knew her, and none could speak reproachfully of her. She had no early advantages, never having been at school a day in her life. By the assistance of her children she learned to read the Bible and hymn-book, in which she took great delight.

The loss of the two little boys left behind in slavery was a great grief. She frequently spoke of them, and wondered where they were, whether dead or alive. Forty-five years rolled away and on their bosom bore her long-absent son Peter to her arms again. She received him with joy, and inquired for the remaining one. " He is dead," Peter replied. She esteemed it a great favor to know of their whereabouts, for she had long despaired of ever seeing or hearing from them again. Like one of old, at this great mercy she was ready to exclaim, " Now lettest thou thy servant depart in peace, for mine eyes have seen thy salvation, and in these latter days beheld the first fruits of my womb." She claimed to be the mother of eighteen children.

On Easter Sunday morning she seemed to be in her usual health, ate a hearty breakfast, and also dinner. Before night she seemed to lose all self-power or control, and we had to help her up-stairs to bed. The power of speech left her, and being asked as to her feelings, whether she was suffering pain or distress of any kind, she informed us that she was not, and that she wanted

nothing.   She seemed perfectly clear in this condition, and remained so several days.   Fearing her
end was drawing nigh, I wrote to all of the brothers and sisters, telling them that if they wanted to
see their mother again whilst alive they must come
without delay.   This they all did, with one excep-
tion.

By this time she had regained her speech suffi-
ciently to talk with them, and to let them know
that death was no terror to her.   Her sky was
clear, her sea was calm, her hope was in the great
I AM, and when she came near to the Jordan its
waters did not affright her.   She knew and felt
that 'twas the way the holy prophets went to in-
herit the heavenly land promised by the Great
King of the country where sorrow and sighing are
unknown, and where the inhabitants shall no more
say, " I am sick."   Yes, where her babes had preceded her, and at the right hand of God kept the
reward of all her prayers and tears.   On the
twenty-third day of April, eighteen hundred and
fifty-seven, her happy spirit left its tenement of clay
and returned to God, who gave it.

After her departure we made the necessary preparations to deposit her remains by the side of her

husband, our father, on the old homestead. The day appointed drew forth a large concourse of friends and acquaintances to view the last remains. We laid her away in the earth to sleep until the resurrection morn.

CHAPTER XIII.

In the spring of eighteen hundred and sixty-one, as I have previously said, I paid off all my debts, and consequently was feeling more easy in financial matters. My revenue seemed to be increasing; my practice, too, was more than I could attend to, and my success, perhaps, was equal to the best. I rode every day to see my patients, allowing myself two hours in the day to attend to those who called at the office. I would generally stay at home on Sundays, to rest myself and horse, but I soon found it to be the most trying day of all others.

As persons knew I would be there, they came from all quarters with all kinds of diseases. Often on that day I have had fifty persons call on me. Frequently I would not have time to eat my meals, and this proved damaging to my health. By strict application to business, with a determined will to succeed, I found my health declining very much, and I knew well that I wanted recreation, but I saw no way to get it. I continued on as best I could, the people seeing my success in practice and knowing well that I had not run it into the ground, as some had prophesied. My merits were freely discussed, some claiming that I was a benefactor to mankind, some extolling me highly, saying there was none like me in all kinds of diseases, and others contending that I knew nothing except to treat sores and the like. The physicians now and then would acknowledge in me a skill in treatment of sores, but would say that I knew nothing of fevers.

Sometimes I heard that Doctor B. would remark by way of derision, on learning of my being to see some of his patients, " Oh, they will soon be well now; black Jim has been there!" I observed, too, in coming in contact with some of the medical gentlemen, that their peacock-feathers would fall, certainly for nothing I had done to them, but perhaps it was for something I might do for their patients that their own skill could not do.

I was frequently reminded of the diamond and the loadstone in the fable. At a certain time there was a diamond of great beauty and lustre observing not only many other gems of a lower class ranged together with him in the same cabinet, but a loadstone likewise placed not far from him. He began to question the latter as to how he came there, and what pretensions he claimed to be ranked among the precious stones,—he who appeared to be no better than a mere flint, a sorry, coarse, rusty-looking pebble, without the least shining quality to advance him to such an honor; and concluded by desiring the loadstone to keep his distance and pay a proper respect to his superiors.

"I find," said the loadstone, "you judge by external appearance, and condemn without due examination, but I shall not act so ungenerously by you. I am willing to allow you due praise. You are a pretty bauble, and I am mightily delighted to see your glitter and sparkle. I look upon you with pleasure and surprise, but I must be convinced that you are of some sort of use before I acknowledge that you have any real merit, or that I treat you with that respect which you seem to demand. With regard to myself, I confess my deficiency in outward beauty, but I may venture to say that I make amends by my intrinsic qualities. The great improvements of navigation are owing to me. By me the distant parts of the world have been made known and accessible to each other. Remotest nations are connected, and all, as it were, unite in a common society. By mutual intercourse they relieve one another's wants, and all enjoy the blessings peculiar to each. The world is indebted to me for its wealth, its splendor, and its power, and the arts and sciences are in a great measure obliged to me for their improvements and their continual increase. Of all these blessings I am the origin, for by my aid is it that man is enabled to construct that valuable instrument, the mariner's compass."

MORAL.

" Let dazzling stones in splendor glare,
Utility's the gem for wear."

CHAPTER XIV.

As it has been so frequently said by physicians that I know nothing of fevers, I feel it incumbent upon me to give a brief sketch of my treatment. It has been always my impression that the doctor was sent for to prevent protraction in disease, and by proper remedies to alleviate the suffering patient. Such being the case, my duty seemed plain. When called to attend a fever patient, I at once set myself to work to find out the nature of the case. I would carefully examine the patient externally and internally. I would pass my hand over the surface of the body to ascertain, if possible, its condition, and in most all cases I found the skin dry and hot, not so much even as finding moisture in the axilla, showing excretions were prohibited from passing through the ordinary channels. Nature makes a charge from within, perspiration attempts to pass, but every avenue is closed. It recedes to the internal organs, and there makes war upon the vitals. The heart is compelled by the invader to resist powerfully; thus it beats one hundred and ten or more. The pulse is an indication of what is going on. The patient is thirsty and racked with pain. The head seems ready to burst, the eyes glare, the tongue is coated, the breath offensive, the urine scanty, and every function deranged. Appetite gone, sleep disturbed and unrefreshed, watchers begin to prognosticate for good or bad.

Now for treatment. I first ordered my patient to be bathed all over with soda-water or weak lye, the whole surface to be rubbed well with it. Next sudorific medicine, followed with warm catnip tea, to be repeated two or three times a day. If the head be hot, take whisky, vinegar, and soft water (one teacup of each), and one teaspoonful fine salt; mix, and apply cold several times a day. Soak the feet at night in ashes and warm water. Give a dose of vegetable physic every day, or every other day, according to circumstances. Keep up a determination to surface. Give a portion of diaphoretic powders at night, followed with warm catnip tea, to promote sleep. Wash the face, chest, and arms with vinegar and water every day. Give cold water, if craved, or plenty of lemonade, made in the usual way. If vomiting take place, take one teaspoonful of saleratus, put in half-pint of peppermint tea, and sweeten with white sugar, and give a tablespoonful to an adult every fifteen or thirty minutes, till the vomiting stops. Add ten drops of laudanum to each dose, and for low excitement or prostration take carbonate of ammonia (hartshorn) three scruples, gum-arabic and loaf sugar each two drachms, mint tea half-pint, mix, and give one table-spoonful or two every hour, according to circumstances. If the tongue is much coated, or the symptoms do not change for the better, give an emetic, composed of vegetable, followed by warm boneset tea, to be drank freely to assist vomiting ; this will cleanse the stomach and excite perspiration.

If this treatment be strictly followed, you shall not need to wait nine days for the fever to run its course. Beside, you shall find that the name of the fever is not such a monstrous matter as that you read of in the books of allopathy, and as you have been led to believe.

I will give now some recipes which I think are

very valuable in treating fevers and many other maladies:

SUDORIFIC DROPS.

Take Opium	.	.	.	.	2 oz.
Ipecac	.	.	.	.	2 "
Saffron	.	.	.	.	2 "
Camphor		.	.	.	2 "
Virginia snakeroot	.		.		2 "
Pleurisy root	.		.	.	2 "

All bruised; diluted alcohol, 3 quarts.

Place these in a bottle and macerate for two weeks, then express, and filter through paper; or if you have a percolator you can put the bruised articles in it and pour on alcohol to cover them, and let them stand for twenty-four hours, then gradually pour on the rest of the alcohol, until it all runs through in a bottle to receive it.

Dose.—One teaspoonful in a teacupful of warm catnip tea every hour or two till it produces perspiration.

This I have found to be one of the best remedies in fulfilling the intention for which it is given; which is, generally, to produce free perspiration. One dose or two, aided by warm catnip tea, and bathing the feet in warm water and ashes, will cause copious perspiration. Hence it is useful in many diseases, as fevers, pleurisy, inflammation, colds, and coughs.

EMETIC POWDER.

Take Ipecac   .   .   .   .   4 oz.
Lobelia .   .   .   .   4 "
Bloodroot   .   .   .   2 "

Pulverize separately, mix, and rub well in a mortar.

Dose.—Teaspoonful given every thirty minutes in warm boneset tea. Useful in all cases where an emetic is required.

It is not often the second dose is required to produce the effect desired. Thus you cleanse the stomach, dislodge morbific matter, excite the viscera, vivify the nerves, open the pores, and drive the invading disease from the vital parts and places, and leave the enemy at the mercy of the practitioner.

ANTIBILIOUS POWDERS, OR COMMON PHYSIC.

Take Jalap root, pulverized   .   4 oz.
Alexandria senna, pulverized 8 "

Cream of tartar	. .	½ oz.
Cloves, pulverized .	.	3 drs.

Mix, and rub well in a mortar.

Dose.—One teaspoonful in warm water, sweetened, on an empty stomach.

This I think is one of the best medicines used as physic. It cleanses well the stomach and bowels, and is not drastic in its operation; is perfectly safe to persons of all ages, from the infant of one week old to the old man of one hundred years. It removes viscid accumulations in a surprising manner, and restores the enervated powers of nature.

Cough Balsam.

Take Spikenard root	. .	8 oz.
Comfrey root .	. .	8 "
Horehound tops	. .	8 "
Elecampane root	. .	8 "
Bloodroot	. . .	8 "
Skunk-cabbage root	.	8 "
Pleurisy root .	. .	8 "

All bruised; then boil in two gallons of soft water down to one gallon; express and strain the liquid, and see that you have one gallon. Then add ten pounds of white sugar, and boil to form a syrup. When done, strain again into something to cool, and when nearly cool take two drachms oil anise and four ounces alcohol, mix and pour into the balsam; also one pint tincture of lobelia. Let the whole stand twenty-four hours to settle, then bottle up in half-pint bottles.

Dose.—One teaspoonful three, four, or five times a day.

This balsam far excels anything that I have ever known used for pulmonary affections and coughs of long standing. It is admirably calculated to relieve that constricted state of the lungs which is so often met with in consumption. It assists expectoration and invigorates the whole system, and is seldom or never given without benefit. This is an excellent remedy for asthma or any bronchial affection attended with difficulty of respiration.

It will be observed that the doses mentioned in these recipes are for adults, and may be proportioned to children according to their age. In giving my early recollections, I did not propose, in the first place, to add to the account any of my recipes, or to give the history of my treatment of fevers or any other diseases ; but, being a firm believer in the gift of Providence, I could not well omit it, knowing that all mankind owe their being to that Creator who bestows his blessings upon all.

He it is who supplies the head with brains, the heart with thought according to that we are capacitated to receive, and much depends on ourselves whether we advance in knowledge or recede into idiocy. For myself, I very much regret that I did not enjoy the advantages of an early education. I had but six months of schooling, and that under very imperfect teachers. I beg, therefore, the pardon of my readers for errors in this work.

When I take a retrospective view of my life, of the many difficulties with which I have had to contend, the mountains of prejudice which I have had to meet, the poverty which hung as a dark cloud about my childhood and early manhood, without training, a mind uncultivated and undisciplined, no one to lend a helping hand, but many to give the cold shoulder and hinder my progress as best they could, I almost wonder that I have attained my present time of calm weather and clear sky. All the blessings and many of the luxuries of life surround me, and as I humbly trust I have served in some measure the genera- tion to which I belong, I can only exclaim, " He that is mighty hath done great things for me."

In this retrospect I take great consolation. As my warfare here is nearly over, I feel content to ground arms and leave the field for enrolment on the retired list of the superannuated. Although my time may be brief, I have the pleasant satisfac- tion of knowing that I have aught against none and good-will to all. Man is as a shadow that soon passeth away, and he will be known no more. Though he have millions of gold, with houses and lands in abundance, though he be able to say, " I am monarch of all I survey," yet time with relent- less swiftness rolls him into eternity. Though he pride himself upon his knowledge and refinement, though he claim the honor of collegiate, with long lists of diplomas, yet his body must return to the earth, and his spirit unto the God who gave it.

The laws of nature are justly executed. The rich, the poor, the learned, the unlearned, the king who rules a nation, or the beggar upon the wayside, all meet on the common level of hu- manity at the grave. One, the mighty One from the beginning, claims the power to execute justice, and all have to submit, and none can escape His eternal fiat, "Dust thou art and unto dust thou shalt return."

CHAPTER XV.

In the year of eighteen hundred and sixty-two I was called to attend Ann Wilkins, with whom I served my time. I went to see her, but administered nothing, for reasons which I need not mention here. The poor woman's sufferings from the first of January up to the eleventh of May, when death came to relieve her, were very great. Although the best medical aid had been employed, it was of no avail. Let family ties be what they may, the grim monster Death knows no compassion. Notwithstanding the desolation of sons and daughters, the bereavement of the husband of a companion and the neighbors of a friend, the life of Ann Wilkins ended, and her spirit took its flight. I was notified of her funeral, which I attended. Was it not remarkable that she should send for me in her illness, and be willing to confide her life in the hands of one whose life had contended with so many disadvantages? What it

was that gave her confidence, I will leave the
reader to answer, but to me it seemed the leading of that Providence whose finger had ever
been guiding my way.

> What little knowledge I have gained,
> Was all from simple nature drained;
> Hence my life's maxims took their rise,
> Hence grew my settled hate to vice.

On the nineteenth day of August, eighteen hundred and sixty-two, I had been to attend a patient
in Shamong, and as I was returning home by way
of Huckleberry Mount, driving slowly along, musing over the past and congratulating myself upon
the present, I chanced to look on my right, and
there beheld a large rattlesnake. My first thought
was to kill it. I prepared a stick and approached
it in a warlike attitude, intending that my first
stroke should despatch the reptile. I raised my
stick, tightly grasped with both hands, and with
great vehemence made a stroke, but missed my
aim. I stepped back, looked at it, and concluded
to capture and take it home alive. I knew that I
was risking my life if I failed to accomplish my
end, yet felt sure that I had the antidote with me

if it should happen to be more exact in aiming a blow than I. So I renewed the attack on his snakeship with paper in one hand and stick in the other. I made a sure pass this time, and dealt a blow a few inches from the head, which caused it to rage and rattle furiously. I threw the paper down, and, with the stick, turned his head upon it, held it there, and enveloped the head in the paper. I tied it with a string, put it in my carriage, and took it home. When there, I placed it on the floor of the office and called my neighbors and family in to see it. It continued to move round for four or five hours, all in good plight, except the head, which it could not move.

After we had tired looking at it, I concluded to put it into a large glass bottle filled with alcohol, supposing it would die instantly or within three or five minutes. I was disappointed to see it moving round in the spirits for nearly two hours, the last moments of which it seemed to be in terrible anguish, exerting every effort to free itself, but could not, and finally sank to the bottom. At the expiration of thirteen years it retains its natural appearance, and is in good state of preservation.

I was always fond of curiosities, and made them

an object of special attention. I have collected some, and have them in my possession. A pig with one head, four ears, and two bodies and eight legs, I have been keeping, with alcohol, for over thirty years in a glass bottle. I have a number of Indian relics, some things manufactured by them from stone, such as axes, pestles, hammer-heads, skinning-knives, arrow-heads or spears, shoe-lasts, and other things that were made in the stone age by that strange people.

At leisure times I occupied myself by skinning and stuffing birds and animals in a way original with myself. Taxidermy was like, to me, all other scientific branches; I knew it to be obscured by those who possessed the knowledge; therefore, I considered, if the man is dead who first accomplished it without information, there may be some one living in this age who can do something similar. I succeeded pretty well in it, for I was always determined to accomplish what once I undertook.

It was a great pleasure to me to go botanizing over the fields and meadows and through the wood and along the creeks. For hours I would be absorbed in studying the nature of the plants and their medical properties. A good botanical book was usually my company and my sympathizing, entertaining, helpful friend.

During the years of eighteen hundred and sixty-three and four I have but little to narrate, except my practice, which was extensive, and embraced all manner of diseases common to this part of the country. I rode day and night, and through all weather. Beside, I had an extensive office practice. I made it a purpose to be at home about the middle of the day, and often there would be six or eight carriages waiting my return. There was the infant of a few weeks old and the man of ninety years. It actually seemed to me that old people came to me half believing that I owned the fabled fountain of perpetual youth, and could help them in infirmities that age had brought upon them. So I used to say to them, "It is of God's mercy only that you are yet alive and able to tell of your aches and pains. Old age I know not how to prescribe for." Nevertheless, I prescribed for them such remedies as I thought best for their advanced years, and some of them sometimes claimed to have received great benefit from the treatment.

I never offered any inducements, either verbal or written, for persons to try my remedies. I was willing to let merit alone be the test, and parties left free to choose or to refuse as best suited them. I always had a special abhorrence of those who vaunted themselves and medicines as superior to any other. It was to me like a net cast into the sea for fish, the small and weak getting caught and the large making good an escape. The millions of money expended in vaunted remedies by the sick, in hopes of being relieved of their ills, cannot be estimated. The venders of quack nostrums eat the oysters and the afflicted the shells.

As to specific medicines, I have not found them. Although I have found medicine that would seem to be suited to many people for the same disease, it has again been rejected by others apparently under the same conditions. Different constitutions require different remedies to accomplish like results, therefore, I know no specific remedies.

If specific remedies were available under all conditions, there would be no trouble in the practice of medicine. Just keep them on hand, and administer when needed, and the patient would soon be convalescent, and no fear that the cranium of the practitioner would burst with the resources of knowledge he was obliged to keep stored there.

It has always been my delight to prepare my own medicines. This has been a branch of my business to which I have devoted much time. I prepared everything I used, whether pills, powders, syrups or tinctures, salves or ointments. By this means I had the pleasant satisfaction of knowing what I was giving to my patients, and I always knew it to be a good and pure article.

Part of my time I studiously devoted to reading anatomy and physiology. My studies, together with my practice, made my life a busy one. Often I have felt the keenness and the responsibility of being alone in my profession; no one with whom to hold conference or to cheer or comfort me when depressed with difficult cases. Human beings, like plants, thrive best by being cultivated. It is easily conceived what a vast amount of good may be done by the association of good friends. The mind is strengthened, gloomy fears are dispelled, the faculties enlightened, and troubles calmed. Of all these social gifts I have been deprived. Men stand on their merits, and rise and fall among their fellows by the linkings and attritions of social life. The best wick in the best lamp without oil gives but a feeble light, and that of short duration.

The vine of the forest that has no support is compelled to trail on the ground, subject to being trampled upon; and why does it not climb? There is nothing within reach that it can lay hold of. If you assist it by placing a pole securely by its side, you will soon see it leave its humble position and cling to and ascend the pole to a more sublime one, where its beauties are all displayed.

The once humble vine that was barren is now prolific, its branches hanging with clusters of the choicest fruit that excite the admiration of all who behold it; whereas before its upclimbing it had no charms, no clusters, and no notice was taken of it except it happen to entangle one's feet, when execrations would be visited upon it. How changed! Refined gentlemen visit it, ladies admire it, and with their soft hands pluck its clusters and desire to be protected from the scorching rays of the sun by its branches. Birds chirp on its twigs, the sun vivifies it, the clouds of heaven, water it, the air is made fragrant by its perfume, and nature seems to smile upon her own production.

CHAPTER XVI.

I HAVE here a word to say to young men who have been deprived of early advantages of education, those who have felt the stirring of faculties within them equal to or perhaps superior to those of their more favored fellows. There are unprincipled men who would set you at naught, and make you believe that your head and brain were only of chance, that you were to be of little use among your fellows except as a menial. From these influences you may be driven to dissipation and despair. Or should you be so fortunate as to rise above your condition, become the means of new discovery in science or thought, these very same men, while they despise you as the medium, will appropriate your discovery, and claim for themselves the honor that belongs to another.

Nature teaches the truest philosophy. You have, young man, brains that were given you by God, the author of all good gifts. He has en-

132

dowed you with thinking powers. All men like the esteem of their fellows, and this may be brought about by energy, honesty, and upright deportment. Shun the society of the lewd; there is nothing to be gained from them but vice and poverty. Do not allow yourself to be enticed to the gambling-house, where the mind becomes dwarfed and hardened against what is good and great. Shun the tippling-houses. Treat all men with decorum. Be assiduous in all your undertakings. Fulfil your promises to the letter. Read instructive books, among which the Bible is first. Be unassuming in your manners. Turn a deaf ear to those who call you a fool for your pains, and discourage you from attainment. Press forward, the prize is before you and *for you*.

Although your sky may often be clouded, the sun will shine forth in the end, and its rays brighten your road to victory. Do not speak disparagingly of your neighbors. Treat your enemies with all the courteousness you can command. Use no profane language,—beside being debasing to the soul, it is not the mark of a gentleman. Let not worldly riches be your chiefest goal, for you cannot take them with you when you exchange time for eternity. Be frugal in all things. Help the needy. In jesting, be careful to use no words that shall wound or offend. Be neat in your person and apparel. Do no work on the Sabbath day, as it is strictly forbidden in the Bible. Avoid going to law with your neighbors; settle your difficulties, if possible, by compromise.

Buy only such things as you need. Do not think you ought to have everything you see your more able neighbor have. Never allow yourself to forget a debt. Remember your own obligations to others as you remember the obligations of others toward you. Study attentively the laws of nature, which are the source of all knowledge. Follow the precepts which I have here inculcated, and you will be honored in your life and in your death. Worthy men will esteem it an honor to be counted among your friends, and God Himself will bless you.

Young women, too, I have a word for you. By the restriction of sex you have been hindered in many literary advantages, and schools and opportunities have not opened to you as they have to men. Many of you from an early age have been compelled to work for a living, and to lose yourselves in thoughts and lives of others. Do not allow your lives to become dwarfed, or believe that you are incapable of attainment.

Let me say that God has blessed you with a soul, and with mental powers and activities. Improve the least He has given you for His sake. Shun the company of the lewd. Spend your leisure moments in writing and reading, and in pursuit of those things which make the true lady. Abhor the company of the giddy, from whom you receive nothing but shame. Let not pride have a place in your heart. Be simple in the choice of apparel, and frugal in all things. It seems to me that fashion is like the peacock, which some say has the plumage of an angel, the voice of a devil, and the appetite of a thief; hence, fine feathers do not make fine birds. Apply your mind to profitable study.

Aspire to greatness. Be kind to all. Use no language unbecoming your sex. Learn to read and write your own letters. Do not spend all you earn. Consider that you may be sick or out of employment, and then you will find that your own purse is your best friend. Do not flirt. Do not rejoice at the downfall of one of your sex.

Use your influence to help those who are going
astray. Be modest in all your ways. Avoid
parties and picnics where the rabble congregate;
it is dangerous to your person and injurious to
your morality. Keep private company with the
man whom you love, and no other. Read your
Bible. When you retire at night, commit your
soul unto Him who made you.

Rise in the morning with a cheerful spirit, and
strive to retain it through the day. Shun fortune-
tellers, for they will prejudice your minds against
your best friends. Do not covet your neighbor's
goods. Avoid gossip. Keep your wardrobe neat
and clean. Make yourself an adept in all branches
of housekeeping. Keep your house in order.
Let your gait be modest and graceful. Train
yourself to distinctness of utterance and gentle-
ness of tone.

Should you enter the conjugal state, remember
that it is for life you wed, and to be happy you
must be loving. Be ready gracefully to subdue
any tinge of displeasure or doubt that may arise
in your home. If you become a mother, remember the injunction to " train up a child in the way
he should go, and when he is old he shall not

depart from it." And when old age comes you shall be able to look back upon a well-spent life, and forward to an eternal happy future.

I do not know that I can do better than close this chapter with the allegorical picture of an ideal woman which haunts my imagination. She need not be nameless, for I may call her Mary, from the beautiful name of old. She has moulded her life according to the precepts and examples of virtue, and age finds her honored among her friends, and her soul awaiting its departure.

This Mary is a heroine in everything. At last a messenger is despatched from the country to which she is going, and reads as he approaches her, " I am sent by the King of the Celestial Country, who desires that you lay aside all excuses and appear before Him in white raiment in two weeks from this date; and to confirm what I have said, I herewith leave you a copy of this summons."

He then touches her body with a fever, and bids her be ready. She exclaims,—

> "All is well!
> All is peace and joy divine;
> Heaven and glory, ye are mine."

Informing the family and friends that she has received the message, she makes her will, which reads: To my daughters I give and bequeath my good name, with the charity and graces appertaining thereto, and to my sons I give the gospel admonition, Be wise.

While she is musing in her house, the doors being open to admit air, and two weeks having expired, a messenger enters, makes a low obeisance, and says, "You will pardon me for not knocking; I hope you do remember me, since I was here two weeks ago and summoned you to be ready to appear at the bar of the Chief Judge to give an account of your stewardship here below. My name is Michael;" upon which he touches her heart with his spear, and says, "One hour more and you shall be before the Throne."

Her family gather around, the neighbors come rushing in; they clasp her hand and bid her farewell. She raises her eyes to the skies, folds her hands, and calmly says,—

> "All is well!
> There is no cloud that doth arise
> To hide my Jesus from my eyes;
> All is peace and joy divine;
> Heaven and glory, ye are mine."

There are sighing and mourning and great lamentation; a wife and mother has crossed bold Jordan, and is welcomed by all the heavenly throng. As she enters, they cry, "Sister spirit, from earth come away!"

Her friends prepare her for the tomb: they clothe her in the purest white. As she lies ready for the grave, she looks like an angel. Her friends and neighbors are invited to view her remains and convey them to their last resting-place. The concourse is great, the hearse arrives to convey the body to the tomb; carriages and people clad in mourning gather together. As they move towards the open grave, the sky is clear, the atmosphere serene, the sun shines in all its splendor, and as the procession moves onward even the horses seem to be inspired with the solemnity of the occasion.

We bid farewell to our heroine; she has gone to that city where the inhabitant shall no more say, "I am sick." To the Land of Beulah, where flowers bloom eternally and peace immortal reigns. We are glad to know that some of her offspring yet live and are walking in the path wherein their mother trod.

CHAPTER XVII.

A CASE occurs to my mind of a gentleman who lived about twelve miles from my house. He was taken with erysipelas of the head and face in a very aggravated form. He sent for me to attend him. I did not hesitate for a moment, but went immediately. Arriving at the house a little before noon, I found him sitting in a chair. At first sight I was surprised that a man's face and head could be so distended. I commenced treating by applying a wash, and followed this by application of ointment. I also ordered poultices all over the face and eyes, and gave him physic freely every day or two.

I ordered his feet bathed in warm water, with ashes added, to equalize the circulation. It was astonishing to see the salutary effect it had upon him. I think I paid him five visits, and the man was safely over the violent forms of the disease. After the fever left him every particle of hair came off his head, and he was as bald as a dinner-plate. He wore a wig for some time, and his hair came in again very nicely.

The first visit I paid him was on St. Patrick's day, and I think it was the most terrible storm I ever rode through. It rained, hailed, and snowed. The satisfaction I felt in restoring him to health repaid my drive through the rain, although as a gentleman he paid my bill manfully.

I could enumerate hundreds of cases similar to this, except that none were attended with loss of hair. There was a lady who lived at Medford Glass-works, who, one day, was sweeping off the stove-hearth, which was standing partly on the fire-hearth, when suddenly the hearth gave way. The lady, with the stove, hearth, and kettle of boiling water, went through into the cellar, and she was scalded and burned in a frightful manner.

She was rescued from her perilous condition by her neighbors and family. A physician was sent for, who arrived in good time, but under whose treatment she began to grow worse. After much deliberation on the part of the family, they concluded to send for me. I went at once, found her in a dreadful condition, burned from the abdomen

down to the knees; I might say literally cooked
to the bone. She was suffering excruciatingly, as
though she were held in the fire, without mitigation. The patient was suffering this while the
gloved representative of the faculty was vaguely
hoping that a change would take place for the
better or she be removed by death!

I set at work to relieve her, humiliating as
it may seem to the dignity of the learned
practitioner. I wrapped the affected parts in
poultices, and in a short time reaction took place
and she was relieved. After a few applications of
the poultice,—and I made it my own business to
put them on and take them off,—I noticed in
dressing the flesh that the mortified part came off
with the poultice, leaving nothing but the bone
and the sinews. I continued to treat her case
with external and internal remedies until she
finally recovered, to the great satisfaction of herself and her family, and to the disappointment of
some of my enemies.

I remember the case of a man who unfortunately had a wagon-wheel run over his foot,
which bruised it quite badly. By some misfortune he caught cold in it, which produced inflam-

mation, and was very painful. He sent for Doctor B., who commenced to attend him, but who did not succeed in bringing relief to his sufferings. He at length sent for me. I found him very bad, foot all mortified, and prostration of the whole system. I administered restoratives, and applied a poultice to his foot. Within a few days the dead flesh separated from the living, and the whole top came off, leaving nothing but the bone and sinews, and it was astonishing how soon he recovered.

I will state another case,—that of a man living in Shamong, who had been nursing a friend of his sick with typhoid fever. He caught the fever himself, and was obliged to leave the friend and go home. He sent for me to attend him. I went reluctantly, telling them they had better employ another physician. He seemed to grow ill very fast, and became delirious to such a degree that he did not know that he was sick, and cared neither to live or die. He was driving mules in his delirium, or trading with some one. He had not been sick one week when the sick friend was anxious about him, and sent word to him to get some one else to attend him or I would doctor

him to death. I took no notice of this, but
quietly went on with my duty. I paid the utmost
attention to him, and in less than two weeks he
was able to go out of doors, whilst the friend who
was so able to counsel was confined to his house
for three months. My patient became hale and
hearty, and is living now, twenty years from that
time, while the other never fully recovered his
health, and died several years after. He called
upon me previous to his death, but his constitution was gone, and there was no hope for him.

I think thousands of valuable lives are lost
yearly by the interference and counsel of ignorant
friends, who presume to be wise in matters generally.

The first case of cancer I ever attended was a
lady living near Medford. Her family physician
pronounced it cancer, and said he did not think it
could be cured. She sent for me. I had never
seen a cancer before. I commenced to treat it,
not knowing any cure. I tried several salves, and
finally found the right thing. The affected part
became well, and when it was cured the physician
had the effrontery to say that it was not a cancer,
going back upon his own words. In this case it

was not I (who gave it no name) who said it was cancer, but he; and his judgment must have been faulty either in the first or the last instance; at any rate, he has already gone to meet that God before whom we must all appear, to be judged not according to our education or selfish ambition, but according to honesty and purity of motive.

A young lady came to me at one time from the State of Pennsylvania. I recollect that it was on Sunday, and two carriages drove up filled with representatives of the best blood of the Friends. They came in, and one of them, an elderly lady, introduced the party. She then pressed the old gentleman to ask me any questions in relation to his daughter that he saw proper. He commenced his queries, which, possibly, fell short of a thousand in multitude. I answered as best I could without promising to cure the daughter. I thought the old gentleman used a little more freedom in his questioning on account of my being outside the medical faculty, and also because I was a colored man, which chagrined me, and I concluded to make him pay for his skill in querying.

He told me that his daughter had a cancer on

her eyelid, and wished me to examine it. I did so, and gave no opinion, though I did not think it a very bad case. He knew better what it was than I could tell him. She had been in Philadelphia for the last three months, and had had the advice and consultation of several of the most eminent doctors, who had failed to find a remedy. I thought it strange that after this experience with college-bred physicians the old gentleman should expect me to say at once that I could cure her. I declined giving a positive answer, and said, " I think that I can do it."

At this, one of the ladies, who was acquainted with me, said, " We like Dr. Still all the better for answering in that way; it shows he makes no pretensions. I think he had better try." The father addressed the daughter, and said, " Thou art of age, thou must answer for thyself." It was proposed, and soon agreed upon, that she should board at the house of the lady who had introduced them, and all things being settled, in a few moments I applied a plaster to the parts affected, which acted like a charm. I attended her at her boarding-place for two or three weeks, and at the end of that time she was well, and went to Philadelphia to attend Yearly Meeting, and her friends and relatives congratulated her on being so marvellously cured.

Notwithstanding all this, these same physicians who had first pronounced judgment upon her case swallowed their own words, and said it was not a cancer. It looks to me as though they told untruth first or last, as I only doctored it for what they called it; I myself never gave it a name.

I might fill volumes of just such cases as above stated, where I have cured patients who have been pronounced incurable in cancers, tumors, white-swelling, and almost every kind of disease, which fact has led me to believe that all diseases are curable in certain states or conditions of them, and I cannot believe otherwise. Thirty years of practice have confirmed me in this belief. I have attended doctors, lawyers, clergymen, and all other classes of mankind, and have been much gratified to see them restored to health. I can say assuredly that I have found no disease but that I have also found a remedy for it in some stage of it. Strange as this language may seem, it is nevertheless true.

Physicians will tell you otherwise, and when

you read medical works you shall find but few curable diseases laid down in them. These authors claim that disease must run its course; if it terminate favorably, well; and if fatal, that is the way it should go. But why send for a doctor if it is not his business to arrest the disease?

My impression is, and always has been, that the duty of the practitioner is to prevent long or protracted illness and to alleviate suffering. If I am correct in this assertion I trust some one may be benefited thereby.

CHAPTER XVIII.

In July of eighteen hundred and sixty-five my mother's sister, Nancy Washington, died of dry gangrene, which affected her in the toes and feet, and caused great suffering. She lingered some time before death came to relieve her. She was some years younger than my mother, and the last of her sisters who survived her. They had been in life much comfort to each other, and when they met would talk over their young days and tell of the efforts they had made to get free while in slavery.

They often talked, too, of their hardships. They had to work in the field, and plough corn, and all manner of work that men usually pursue. In summer's heat and winter's cold their task was required of them. They were meanly clad. There was no redress for their wrongs, of which they almost regarded it a sin to complain. Their husbands were no protection in their distress, not

daring to utter a word on their behalf. If they did
they would not be allowed to visit them. As was
frequently the case, the husband belonged to one
planter and the wife to another. Therefore the
husbands were constrained to use the utmost
good behavior in visiting their wives, for fear of
being prohibited from visiting them. They lived
mostly on hominy or Johnny-cake; their corn
they had to pound in a mortar at night after
working hours. This made the hominy; and the
cooking was done in their own time, so as to be
ready for the field in the morning.

They also had to live without names, except
such as "Tom," or "Sall," or "Nance," or
"Pete." There was no last name for them, but
they generally were known by the name of their
master, and to most of them it was a boast to be
called by his name. They knew nothing of their
origin further than they could hear some of the
old people communicate traditionally. As to
their ages, they could give no precise date.
Schools to them were more sacred than churches,
as they were allowed to go to church, but to
school never. The more benighted the mind the
better for the master; it made the slave more of

a chattel, or article of trade, by which he could better serve his purpose. They were allowed to sing and dance, as it showed contentment with their condition.

Such was slavery, to which my mother, father, and aunts were subject, and to which a whole race was subject until the Proclamation of Emancipation by the great and good Abraham Lincoln. All those of my kin who served in bondage have passed into that land where equality reigns and where justice is meted to all alike.

In eighteen hundred and sixty-six I was notified to attend the funeral of Amos Wilkins, the man with whom I served my time. To me this was a solemn occasion. I went and viewed for the last time the form of him with whom I had passed my boyhood, and this event forever closed our earthly relation to each other.

He was born July the seventh, seventeen hundred and ninety, in Fostertown, on a farm then owned by his father, whose name was Amos Wilkins. His mother's name was Lydia Jenkins. Amos and Lydia Wilkins had eleven children born to them, one of whom they named Amos, to perpetuate the family name. They were of

Quaker origin. At the death of his father, Amos fell heir to the farm of about ninety acres of land on which he was born. This, without any money, was his portion. He was left to pay his widowed mother an annuity of seventy-five dollars in money, beside other privileges. My old boss, Amos, married Ann Hewlings, and went farming upon the small farm into which he had fallen possession. Both were industrious and thrifty, and they succeeded in accumulating wealth.

He was a man of most even temper. I never heard him find fault, or saw him in a passion. He labored in the field with his men, and used them as he used himself.

He was utterly opposed to lawsuits, and had much rather lose a small sum than go to the trouble of collecting it by law. He was no speculator, was opposed to lending money for a bonus, as he considered it not to be an act of kindness. He was not fond of vain show or fashions of the day. He used no profane language. He never dabbled in other men's matters or political affairs. He knew he was rich, but did not think it made him any better than a poor man. He had nine children, of whom six grew to maturity and five survived him.

For many years he was afflicted with consumption, and in his later life he relinquished labor and gave himself up to study and to religious devotion. He read his Bible and prayed. I was once at his house during his illness when some one came in to pay him interest money, and asked how much it was. He answered, "I don't know; I don't want anything to do with it; it is poor trash, anyway;" so I assisted the daughter and the man to calculate it. He was not, sectarian in his religious views, but attended the churches of various denominations. He died in the seventy-sixth year of his age, leaving a fortune of one hundred and fifty two thousand dollars.

In eighteen hundred and sixty-eight death again made a solemn visit in our family. January tenth of that year my brother Peter died of inflammation of the lungs. His sickness was brief, being only one week from the time he was seized with the attack to the expiration of his suffering.

He had seen very many hardships in his life.

He served in slavery forty-five years, and by saving and industry was enabled to buy his freedom of his master whilst living in Alabama. Having purchased his freedom, he set out toward the North to look for his relations, of whom he knew nothing, and had heard nothing from the time he was five years old. He came to Philadelphia in eighteen hundred and fifty, found his own brother clerk in the Anti-Slavery office there, and from him learned the whereabouts of his mother and brothers. From thence he came to my house, and we took him up to see our mother, whom he had not seen since a small child. After spending a little time among the relatives whom he had never before met, he made up his mind to try to relieve the family whom he had left behind in slavery.

He set his face southward, and, reaching Alabama, told his wife and children of his success in the North, and set about planning to release them. He told them he would send for them, and instructed them how to recognize and receive the messenger should his plans succeed. He bade them a hopeful farewell and came North to consult friends, which he did to a great extent.

Some counselled one way and some another. He gained the sympathy of all who learned his condition.

A gentleman finally volunteered to go and bring his family to him. This person reached Alabama, found those whom he was seeking, and succeeded in conveying them several hundred miles on their way North. He was overtaken, however, by their master, who captured them, carried the slaves back to bondage, and killed the man who had generously volunteered to risk his life in their behalf.

Peter, at hearing this news, was nearly heart-broken. He next purposed to collect money to purchase his wife and children. After travelling about for five years, he gathered the sum of five thousand dollars, with which he bought them. They were delivered to him in eighteen hundred and fifty-five, the wife, two sons, and a daughter. They arrived at my house on January thirteenth of that year, and after showing his family to anxious friends who were interested, Peter settled down with them in Burlington, New Jersey.

There he purchased a small truck-farm of ten acres, and had a house and other buildings erected thereon. He commenced farming and trucking, selling his produce in the town, where he was patronized by many of the best families, who sympathized with him on account of his past condition, and thus was enabled to provide a living for himself and family. He left his property to his wife during her life, and at her death to pass to a son and daughter.

CHAPTER XIX.

I REBUILT my house in eighteen hundred and sixty-nine. I made it forty feet front and twenty-six feet deep, with dining-room and kitchen back, with Mansard roof, water-works, and all the modern improvements, which was the first building of the kind in our neighborhood. Although it was attended with an expense of several thousand dollars, I was able to meet it. I hired my workmen by the day, and paid them every Saturday night, so when the last nail was driven and the last stroke struck I was ready to pay the last dollar.

This I considered a great change in the affairs of life; a mighty stride indeed for one who encountered only poverty, opposition, and prejudice from the beginning. I claim that truthfulness and energy are the weapons that enable us to surmount all difficulties in life, and subdue our enemies and make us prosperous and happy. In all of prosperity that has been given me I have been careful not to choose pride as my companion, although there have been times when I could not refrain from looking into the past, and, comparing it with the present, have been constrained to say, " He that is mighty hath done great things for me."

Previous to rebuilding my house, in the year eighteen hundred and sixty-seven, I made a purchase of a lot of cedar swamp of Lemuel Prickett, for the sum of three hundred and fifty dollars, in what is called Bear Swamp, in Southampton Township; also, a lot of woodland in Shamong Township, of C. and B. Shreve, for three hundred and sixty dollars; also, a lot of meadow and upland, of nine or ten acres, formerly belonging to Joshua Stokes, for the sum of two thousand two hundred dollars. For all of these purchases I paid cash at the delivery of the deeds.

I merely mention these transactions to show the results of my business and the way I conducted matters generally. It has often been said that colored men do not know how to appreciate or appropriate money. I have tried to live so as to prove that the race is capable of a great many things, and I would like to be an example to my sons, and all other poor young men who shall be so unfortunate as I was to have to commence the battle of life without education or pecuniary means.

The race is not to the swift or the battle to the strong, but to those who honestly contend until the warfare is ended.

There was another purchase which I had nearly forgotten to mention, and that was the Town House property as it was called. I bought this in eighteen hundred and sixty-eight, for two hundred and eighty dollars, of the Township Committee, at a public sale. This property lay right in my other land. It consisted of an acre, with a one-story brick-house which had been built upon it for a Town Hall many years previously.

I accomplished these things beside sustaining my family and endeavoring to school my children. This latter subject was one of deep concern to me, for I remembered my own early disadvantages. I endeavored to keep them in school all I could, and succeeded pretty well while they were small, but when they grew to a larger size the teacher treated them with a coldness common in white schools. They were sometimes looked upon as inferior beings. I was sending them to a school near by, taught by a neighboring young man, and I supposed all was well, but the young man discovered eventually that he was not doing the will of God in teaching colored children, so he repented for what he had done, and resolved to sin no more. Consequently, my children had to quit the school. His bills were paid always when presented, and I was sorry that my children lost the instruction of a worthy young man. Yet such have been the times we have lived in.

CHAPTER XX.

In the year eighteen hundred and seventy, I think, I extended an invitation to all of my brothers and sisters to meet at my house on a certain day, that we could enjoy each others' presence in our old age and talk over our past childhood, when we used to play together on the green sward, the time when we knew no cares.

Finally, the appointed day came, and with it the invited guests. I think it will not be out of place to name them, beginning at the oldest sister, —Mahalah Thompson, and her husband, Gabriel Thompson; my widowed sister, Kitturah Willmore; brother Samuel Still; sister Mary Still, who was never married; Charles W. Still, never married; William Still, author of the "Underground Railroad," and his wife. This composed the company.

As this was the first gathering of the kind that occurred amongst us, a seriousness seemed to pervade the little assembly. We talked over the past and looked on each others' cheeks, all furrowed over with age. We spoke of the future, and all professed to have a hope of meeting each other in a better land.

We could only congratulate each other on our present good health in our old age, and to think that seven of us brothers and sisters, out of eighteen, were now blessed to meet together to partake of a bountiful repast.

Although none of us were tipplers, I uncorked a bottle of currant wine that I had made some ten years previous, and we all joined in expressing it to be the best that we had ever tasted. None of us felt that we were connoisseurs in the art of wine-praising, but we all felt satisfied to give it the praise.

It was indeed a day of enjoyment to all. Each one had some little anecdote to relate about the past, calling to recollection some little incident that had long faded from the memory of the rest, even so far back perhaps as half a century.

We talked of father and mother, and their many hard struggles both in and out of slavery, and their strict discipline in the family. We all were grateful to think that it was for our good, and that we were now in a measure reaping the reward of their prayers and labor. God forbid that we should be negligent to their admonitions !

We also talked of the emancipation of the slaves in the United States by Abraham Lincoln. "Is it possible," said we, "that we are living in a land where slavery has ceased to exist?" In this we all rejoiced greatly.

We would ask each other the question, "Did you expect to live to see this day?" We could only say the Ruler of the Universe saw that it was enough and interposed, and who can stand before Him ? So we gave honor to whom honor was due, but we felt to say, "Give God the praise, for He is mighty, and who can prevail against Him ? When He speaks by his thunderings, all the human family, with the beast of the forest, together with all that dwells in the seas, tremble at his voice !"

The day of our meeting was gliding along and the sun advancing to the western horizon, admonishing us to prepare to bid each other adieu and repair to our several homes with all the good cheer we could command. We clasped each others' hands with tears in our eyes, and bade adieu, supposing it to be the last meeting of the kind that we should enjoy this side of eternity, and each one repaired to his and her home to consider that the best of friends must part.

I hope the reader will be able to realize our feelings on this occasion. To us it was a day of great enjoyment. The sun shone in all its brilliancy, and everything seemed serene beyond expression. We can only say,—

> The great God that rules on high
> And all the earth surveys,
> To Him alone we render thanks
> And everlasting praise.
>
> The God who rules with majesty—
> His care is over all ;
> He knows the number of each hair,
> And every sparrow's fall.
>
> Though man possess ten thousand fields,
> And banks of glittering gold,
> He's naught but chaff before the wind ;
> And by the Lord controlled.

CHAPTER XXI.

In May, eighteen hundred and seventy-two, I commenced to remodel and to build to the Town Hall, to make of it tenement-houses. It had constituted one room of thirty-eight feet square, the walls being of brick. I had the old roof taken off, a Mansard one substituted therefor, the one room apportioned into rooms, and a new addition of thirty-six by sixteen feet built back for dining-rooms and kitchens. When completed there were two snug dwelling-houses of seven rooms each. This I did at a cost of about two thousand five hundred dollars.

In the spring of eighteen hundred and seventy-two I found I was much broken down by being overtasked with business, and concluded to give up my outside practice and continue only that which came to my office, hoping to regain my former health. It proved a delusion, and in August of that year my wife and myself went to

Long Branch and stayed four days. When coming home I thought that I felt much better. As we left the cars five or six persons joined me to go up to the office for medical attendance. It was about four o'clock in the afternoon. When I reached the house I found my office full, waiting my return. These patients, in addition to those accompanying me, occupied my time several hours, and when I retired for the night I found myself drifting back into the very condition in which I was upon leaving home.

My short respite was of no avail. I would gladly have relinquished my labor a longer time, but there seemed no way in which I could do it. I continued as best I could with my office work, suffering continually from great prostration. This physical condition continued for more than a year. About the middle of December, eighteen hundred and seventy-three, on arising one morning as usual, I found that I could not stand, or put my left foot upon the floor. It was sore and painful. Dressing myself carefully, I trusted that the pain and soreness would pass away, but it seemed to increase in severity upon my stirring about, and in a few moments became intolerable.

Attempting to go down-stairs, I found that I could not suffer my foot to touch the floor, and managed to get to the dining-room upon my hands and knees. By the help of a crutch and a cane I succeeded in reaching the office, and there applied various soothing applications, which were without avail.

The pain was located in the bottom of the foot, and harassed me with the most extreme torture. The pain of amputation could scarcely have exceeded it. In a few days I was much prostrated by the loss of sleep and appetite. My neighbors seemed alarmed, and many kind friends came to my room to see me. One person came twice a day, and urged strongly that I send for a physician. I objected, well knowing what any would prescribe me, so I continued to treat my own case. From the bottom of the foot the pain ascended the leg, where there was no alleviation. After thus suffering a week, I was attacked with pleurisy in the right side. At this I felt my days to be numbered, and, with no fears of the future, resigned myself to death.

After suffering for some weeks, with surprise to myself I began to amend. The pain subsided, and appetite became improved. Many people told me they shed tears for me and offered up prayers for my restoration. To the many kind friends who came at the time to see me, and sympathized deeply with me in my suffering, I am under lasting obligations. I have been told that I was daily inquired after at all the railroad stations and public places; that there were those who mourned my death as a public calamity; and that it was currently supposed that I was dead, which supposition the editor of the " Mirror" reported differently.

Apart from the seriousness of death, it is amusingly interesting to yet be upon this mundane sphere and to know what, in the event of one's "shuffling off this mortal coil," his fellow-men have to say of him. One pleasant thought came to me in my suffering, and as I felt my own departure to be near, and that was that I had charity toward all and ill-will to none. Although I had never been sick before, I felt surprised that I survived the stroke, and I came to the conclusion that if I continued to improve I would do but little business.

In this I was disappointed. As soon as it was known that I was about again I was fairly besieged with patients, to whom I gave my utmost attention.

This seemed to weigh heavily upon me, and as spring and summer drew on, though not utterly prostrate, I did not recover my wonted animation. I did as little as possible, well realizing that money was no substitute for health.

CHAPTER XXII.

I RECOLLECT a case of a young lady, a Miss
———, of Jacobstown, about seventeen years of age,
who, with her parents, called on me to be treated
for a tumor under the ear. I made different applications of plasters, which did not seem to have
the desired effect. I gave her medicine and ad-
vised her to have patience for awhile; not to be
rash; and, above all, not to submit to an operation
by the knife. "If you do," I said to her, "it will
kill you." I counselled the father and mother and
grandfather to the same effect.

Fortunately, or unfortunately, a neighboring physician learned of the case, and fearing his scientific popularity was in danger of receiving a blow
from honesty and truthfulness, at once (I have been
informed) interfered. He said to the father, "Why
are you taking your daughter to Medford, to that
old nigger? He will kill her. Take her to Philadelphia, to Dr. ———; he will cut it out in five

minutes, and make a job all right." The father demurred, but the physician insisted, and succeeded in drawing him into his net. The young lady went to Philadelphia as instructed, submitted to the cutting operation, and what was the result? Within ten days she was laid away in the tomb.

You may imagine you see the fond mother almost in convulsions to learn that her daughter is no more. Her screams are loud and uncontrollable; her grief is intolerable; her tears flow like streams from a fountain. The father's grief was also great, but he calmed his own sorrow to assuage as best he could that of the wife and mother. It was a heart-rending scene to think that the five minutes' work was the cause of their daughter's death!

Neighbors sympathized, relatives wept and mourned, but all in vain. I suppose the doctor who counselled the father to have it done felt happy to think it was or was not done scientifically by "the old nigger at Medford," as he expressed it. Let me say thousands are carried to their graves annually just from the meddling of good friends, who, like the physician referred to, presume to know more than any one else.

The reader may suppose that I felt quite chagrined when I heard of the doctor's vociferations against me.   Certainly I never claimed any superior skill or knowledge, never induced persons to try my remedies, either by circulars, cards, or advertisements, or any other way. I left parties free to choose for themselves. If they chose to call upon me I felt free to treat them honorably, and in the face of great opposition by the learned doctors.   I had all I could attend to.

I had one thing to console me, and that was these great men die like those whom they take pleasure in deriding, and their memory perishes with them.   I said "great" men, I should have said all men, the noble and the ignoble.   All alike are summoned to the bar of justice to face that Being who knows no prejudice, and a refulgence which was their lot, I fear, shall be blacker than midnight darkness.

It seems to me if such only had it in their power they would dethrone Almighty God and establish a new order of mankind generally.   It seems to me that the tenth verse in Jude is very applicable to their case, but these "speak evil of those things which they know not; but what they know naturally as brute beasts, in those things they corrupt themselves."

Oh, how wonderfully sublime men would be if only they would cultivate that natural relation designed by the Creator! But it seems to me a prevailing custom for man to envy his fellow-man and degrade him all he can.

How frequently when among men do we hear the expression such an one knows nothing; and it is often said of their superiors, too. Forgetting at the same time that they are walking in a vain show, it is their delight to be vainglorious. Such are never happy in themselves; they are like the troubled sea, constantly casting up mire and dirt. For myself, I will take consolation in that still, small voice which says "Thus far shalt thou go and no farther." "They all do fade as a leaf." Their good deeds are seldom spoken of, but their bad ones often.

I know it was my misfortune to be born poor, and also of that race despised upon American soil in this enlightened nineteenth century; without an education and laboring under many disadvantages; a wide world to rove in, with no one to resort to for protection.

Judge Taney said that black men had no rights that white men were bound to respect. If this thundering exclamation had been uttered against him he would have been like Belshazzar, the king, in Daniel, fifth chapter and sixth verse. His countenance would have changed and his thoughts would have troubled him so that the joints of his loins would have been loosed and his knees would have smote one against the other, and this world to him would have appeared a waste, a howling wilderness.

Whilst I consider these things my heart throbs within me for the fate of those fastuous beings who are passing into eternity before that Judge who careth for the sparrow that not one shall fall without his notice; yes, He who knows the number of the hairs of our head.

It gives me consolation to know that many of the learned and wise men fall into error, and, like king Nebuchadnezzar, call on the magicians and the astrologers to extricate them from their troubles, but all their skill proves a delusion. What next is to be done? Pride must succumb to frailty. They leave the line of popularity and call on an humble Daniel to relieve a troubled heart and to soothe a trembling conscience. The object is accomplished, the king is made glad, then the princes, the presidents, the governors, counsellors, and captains conspire against Daniel to the end that he shall be destroyed from the earth. His mighty wisdom was more than they could endure, and they established a royal statute and made firm decrees that whosoever failed to acquiesce therein should be thrown into the lions' den, there to be devoured by those ferocious beasts.

In this are the wise men again foiled. Daniel receives no hurt either of body or mind. The beasts proved to have more of the love of God than his impious accusers. And what was their fate? By the king's command they were cast into the den of lions, and the lions brake all their bones in pieces or ever they came to the bottom of the den. This story is in the sixth chapter of the book of Daniel.

At one time when my business was rapidly prospering, with great satisfaction to myself and to many others, one evening on receiving my mail I found an envelope enclosing two letters; the first requesting me to send the writer some of my erysipelas remedies, saying that his wife was afflicted with that disease and would like the remedy. He signed his name, but what it was I have forgotten. The second was a very nice little envelope, which, upon opening, gave forth a strange and unpleasant smell. It contained nothing but a powder, the contents of which stifled me. There were persons present who declared emphatically that they, too, were subject to the effect of its fumes, and contended that it was sent to me for my hurt. I am unwilling to believe that any one could be so depraved, and the thing yet remains a mystery.

The reader may imagine that the road of my life has not been always the smoothest. Beset by enemies on every hand, compelled to bear taunts and indignities from those who prided themselves upon glittering generalities, boasting that they knew more than I, because of the education of the schools. For myself I could only answer, no man has taught me. I can only account for success by endeavoring always to be strictly honest in all things,—in medical treatment and in business operations,—and a reliance upon that Divine Being who cares for the sparrow in its flight, and who uses the weak things of the world to confound the mighty. These principles I have endeavored to instil in the minds of my sons. From my mother's knee I have always had a horrible idea of untruth. I have never been able to answer the question why those learned men were not more successful in their treatment of disease. Perhaps it was because a slow cure was best, and failures on their part were not in the count.

A lady in Mount Holly had given birth to a child. For the first two weeks all seemed to go well. At length inflammation of the uterus set in. The physician doing all he could, the lady grew worse. Other physicians were called to no effect; there were no symptoms for the better. The husband became very anxious on account of the wife, and in seven weeks from the beginning of her illness came to me, stated the case, and asked me to go to see her. He told me who was the principal physician (there were three), and, learning that it was one who had always been bitter against me, I declined to go. "Dr. B. will not attend her if he knows I have been there," I said. He insisted upon my going, and was satisfied that Dr. B. should step out, if he chose.

I gave him medicine, and told him that perhaps she would grow better. He took it, went home, and used it. He showed the medicine to the attending physicians, who, not knowing it came from me, said it would be as good as anything. In two days the husband called again, and entreated me to go and see the wife, who wanted to see me very much. I felt deep sympathy for him, but I hesitated extremely to go, for I did not wish to interfere; so I gave him more medicine, and sent him home, hoping that he would not trouble me again.

The next day he returned with dejected countenance and said, firmly, " Doctor, I wish you to go and see my wife;" at the same time giving me a look which I could not resist; " I will take you over and bring you back." I went over in the train on Friday afternoon, took with me such preparations as I thought needful, and on my arrival at the house found the lady prostrate upon the bed. She extended her hand, and, with tears in her eyes, exclaimed, " Oh, doctor, I wish you would do something to relieve me!"

On investigation of the case, I made application to the diseased parts, left medicine, also an external application, gave orders to the nurse how to proceed, bade her good-by, and left. On the following Sunday she was able to sit up and eat some breakfast. The family doctor had called on Saturday morning, and, upon being told that I had visited the house, quietly left, without so much as asking after his patient. Upon a certain occasion the wife of this same physician remarked to a friend of mine, " That black man can't know anything, because he has no education." This was the remark of an Eastern lady with a fair share of education herself, brains small, prejudice and ignorance large.

CHAPTER XXIII.

FEVERS, perhaps, are the largest proportion of the diseases which afflict the human family, and numerous are the experiments and theories on the subject by learned men. Notwithstanding the nature, cause, and treatment are about the same, there seems to be no uniform rule laid down for their treatment that is universally effectual in relieving the patient.

I hope to be pardoned if I am wrong in saying that I do not know an old-school physician who seems to treat fever successfully. They limit it to a certain length of time or number of days. To my mind, a physician is sent for to check disease or to prevent it from running its course. It seems to me there is a lack of medical skill when the patient is told to be still and see what nine days will bring forth. The profession of medicine is the only one in which a man can profit by his blunders and mistakes. Nature, it seems to me, with the nine days' theory, would save the patient much money and suffering.

There is much controversy respecting the causes of fever, but from whatever induced, one thing sure is, that it is an increased action of the heart and arteries to expel from the system morbific or irritating matter. It acts as an invader, and nature makes a charge against it, but not always sufficient to expel. The doctor is sent for to aid nature in her efforts, perhaps in the first symptoms, which are shivering or rigors, followed by a hot skin, a quick pulse, a feeling of languor and lassitude. With such symptoms present there is also loss of appetite, thirst, restlessness, with diminished secretions; indeed, every function is more or less disturbed.

The causes of fever are quite numerous. Indeed, every cause capable of producing a departure from a healthy state predisposes the system to fever. Cold, for instance, plays a very important part. It diminishes the action of the capillary vessels and prevents the exhalants from being thrown off. Thus perspiration is retarded and thrown to the vital organs; the skin becomes dry and hot. Hence the liver, heart, and lungs, and all the internal viscera are overcharged, and the excitement in these parts becomes great. It is the duty of the practitioner to alleviate the sufferings of his patient by proper mode of treatment and suitable remedies.

In the first place, moderate the violence of the arterial excitement and prevent local inflammation and congestion. Support the powers of the system, relieve urgent symptoms, and restore the suppressed evacuations. This will remove the offending or irritating cause, and if this be removed the fever must cease.

In this consists the whole secret of curing fevers in general. In every form of fever it is the duty of the practitioner to render himself an assistant to nature by observing what she is endeavoring to accomplish, in the commencement of the disease,—that is, to expel deleterious matter by the proper passages. It is the duty of art to help nature in her efforts at secretion and excretion of the morbific matter.

The medicines which are proper to be given to assist the secretions are sudorific and diluting medicine, such as produce free perspiration on the surface, evacuate and give a healthy tone to the stomach and whole internal viscera. Thus it is seen that the great secret in curing fevers is the restoration of the secretions and excretions, and as soon as they are restored or perform their office the whole catalogue of symptoms attending on fever at once vanish. When restored to healthy action, how soon convalescence takes place and all the functions of the body become natural. The heat of the system is equalized, the pulse falls to its natural standard, and with the subsidence of the febrile commotion there is healthy action in every organ. The appetite is increased, the strength and health are re-established. Certain it is the stomach has an extensive influence over the whole system, and particularly the skin; therefore if the stomach be disordered the whole system sympathizes. Hence the utility of emetics. In febrile diseases they not only cleanse the stomach of any bilious, feculent, or irritating morbific matter, but, as is often the case, fever is removed by a single emetic. It cleanses the stomach, it excites perspiration, which is of the utmost importance to the fevered patient. Notwithstanding, emetics may be dispensed with and cathartics substituted; although it often happens that one single dose of vegetable emetic will prove of more benefit than half a dozen purgatives, although purgatives are indispensable and must be used in removing feculent matter contained in the bowels, stimulating the exhalant vessels of the mucous membranes of the intestines, causing them to pour out copious effusions from the blood or circulating mass. An immense number of vessels open into the intestines and through their whole extent, from which there is poured out a vast quantity of feculent matter.

When there is a preternatural stimulus given to the intestines by purgations, there is a sympathetic affection of the whole system, the circulation is more equal, the pulse lowered, pain of the head and all other parts diminished, and there is a sensible improvement. In fevers of almost every description it is indispensable to cleanse the stomach and bowels.

I have frequently been delighted with the good effect of an emetic given to patients laboring under intermittent fever. It would act like magic, breaking up the fever at once, and, followed by purgatives and tonics for a short time, the intermittent would not be likely to return.

In intermittent fever the liver, heart, and lungs, and all the internal organs seem to be affected or cease to perform their office; in other words, the whole machine is clogged and requires eliminating to set it in proper running order, which duty devolves upon the practitioner.

The skin has an important office to perform in casting off superfluous and noxious matter; hence it will be seen what mischief must arise from the retention of this perspirable matter, and also what benefit will follow by restoring this secretion. It is of great benefit to fevered patients to keep the skin cool and soft. Here we see the necessity of sudorific medicine, which reduces general excitement, and is the better way of depleting the system; which invariably lessens the force of the heart and arteries by removing from the circulation every agent which is useless or injurious, and by relaxing the constriction of the skin. As soon as perspiration breaks out, there is in febrile patients a mitigation of all the symptoms. The dry state of the skin is removed, the circulation is restored, the fever is cut short just as soon as free sweating takes place. The object of the practitioner, then, should be to restore perspiration and keep up a moisture of the skin. It is a well-known fact that a dry skin is unfavorable, while moisture is favorable. If perspiration cannot be promoted we predict danger; if, on the contrary, it can be promoted and kept up we predict a favorable issue.

Bathing the surface with an alkaline wash I deem one of the best things that can be done for a fevered patient. It has a cooling tendency, lessens excitement, soothes the nerves, and promotes sleep. Indeed, after bathing the change in patient is so great you would almost be led to believe that he had been taking an anodyne.

When attending children in fever, I have ordered them bathed all over with warm, soft water, with a little soda in it. If the fever was high I would have them repeat it two or three times a day, and the effect was surprising. It seemed to obviate the necessity of taking a great amount of medicine. I am aware that this mode of treatment is not popular among the refined class of people; yet human nature is all the same, and should be treated as such.

Cold water is good, and may be drunk when the patient is thirsty. It is really more refreshing than anything else, although I think acidulated drinks, such as lemonade, are also good. Particular attention should be paid to the kidneys. Should they cease to perform their office, or do it imperfectly, the urine will be scanty or much diminished, and is carried into the circulation, where it proves a source of irritation. It is important to restore this secretion by giving diuretic medicine or such as promotes a discharge of urine, which, as soon as promoted, greatly diminishes arterial excitement. It is often the case that fevers are brought to a favorable termination by a spontaneous discharge of this fluid. Bathing the feet also has a salutary effect by equalizing the circulation and recalling the blood to the feet; thereby the pain of the head and other organs is relieved. The best foot-bath, in my opinion, is warm, soft water, with a little sal-soda or wood-ashes added, to give it the consistence of weak lye. The water to be used warm as it can be borne. At the same time drink freely of warm catnip or pleurisy-root tea. Cover up warm in bed, and the next morning take a purgative.

Avoid all violent medicine in fever, such as antimony, mercury, or any other minerals whatever, and also blood-letting, which is sure to disturb the efforts of nature, and induce mischief or disease which will follow the person through life, should they be so fortunate as to recover.

Old fever-sores, as they are called, usually found on the legs, I think, are nothing short of mineral medicine taken into the circulation. I never could comprehend how violent poisons were less deleterious in the hands of a graduate, by him to be given with impunity to all classes of mankind. I have no belief in these old fever-sores, as they are called, for the reason that I have attended a great many fever patients, and I have yet to see the first one with swollen limbs or sore legs after their recovery from fever under my treatment. I think that the proper medicine to be used is vegetable or herb medicine, and the most simple that we can give to fulfil the design for which it was intended.

We should be very cautious how we use or give those deadly poisons to our fellow-man, for it is certain that great numbers of mankind have been deprived of existence and millions of orphans have been made by the champions of those medicines which were intended or designed to relieve the sufferer of his or her ills, and to bring peace and comfort to a distracted family. Thousands have mourned the loss of dear parents or dear children just from the fact of taking those deadly poisons which were ordered or sanctioned by some one of the learned faculty.

We are taught to believe that there is no remedy equal to mercury in liver diseases. Indeed, it is claimed to be a specific in that disease, and almost the first thing administered by the learned faculty. Possibly they know more than I do, or more than I desire to know. My advice to every one is to shun mercury in any form. It causes irritation and inflammation of the internal organs. I have been astonished to see it administered by learned members of the profession, and observed as its result a protruded tongue, swollen gums, loosened teeth, offensive breath, and saliva uncontrollable, with prostration of the whole system. My inference is that the use of so deleterious a poison is unnatural, injurious, and wrong. It induces incurable dropsy, or rheumatism, or ulceration of the lower extremities.

I have found vegetable preparations to be all that could be desired in treating liver diseases.

They eradicate the disease without leaving in their train a list of evils more difficult to cure than the liver complaint itself.

Not long since, a graduate of Göttingen University, Germany, who now lives in Philadelphia, and is a regular practitioner there, called upon me to be treated for what he said was consumption. At our first interview he was much emaciated. His symptoms were, a bad cough, shortness of breath, pulse over one hundred, appetite poor, copious expectoration, and sleepless nights, with sweats. After being in the office a few moments he handed me a letter of introduction. Upon reading it I asked, " Are you Doctor —— ?" to which he answered, " Yes."

In the presence of others he stated how long he had been sick, and what medicines he had been taking, which were Fowler's solution of arsenic and cod-liver oil and tincture of iron. "Don't you know any better than that?" I asked. He answered, " No, sir." " Keep on taking those medicines and they will kill you, if nothing is the matter with you," I said to him imperatively. " I am not taking my own prescriptions," he replied, " but am under treatment of the best physicians in Philadelphia, although I know about them myself."

After further talk I put up medicine for him, and told him to call again in two weeks. On the first visit he had been obliged to ride. At the expiration of a fortnight he came into my office again, accompanied by several other patients, who, with him, had walked from the car station, the distance of about one-half mile.

"Well, doctor, how are you to-day?" I asked, as he sat down. He answered, "Better." "Are you going to get well?" "Yes, sir." "Do not be too sure about that," I said. After some conversation with him he made to me this frank avowal: "I am sorry that I practise what I do, but I know no better." He earnestly solicited me to take him as a student, and said he would do anything I chose to set him at, if I would only instruct him.

"I will keep your office clean and lend you all the assistance in my power."

"It is you, not I, who have the education of the schools. I yearned for knowledge in my youth, but no doors were open by which I might enter into the pleasures of the learned.

What little knowledge I have gained
Was all from simple nature drained."

"Well," said he, "I have as good a diploma as
that of any physician in Philadelphia, and I have
the advantage of consulting with the best of them,
but I cannot live by my diploma, and I further see
that I am not making myself popular by my practice. At the same time, if I adopt any new modes,
yours or any other, I am disowned by the medical
fraternity."

He importuned me considerably for my teaching, but I refused. The same gentleman visited
me several times as a patient, and so recovered his
health that he was able to resume practice.

On one occasion, when at my office, he remarked, " I have never seen so many different and
strange cases as come to you." " I suppose you
saw much more in the hospital," I said; to which
he replied, " Not so many different kinds. They
do not go there, for they are sure they will not be
cured."

This I considered a broad acknowledgment for
a member of the Faculty to make,—one boasting
a diploma from a German university.

CHAPTER XXIV.

RHEUMATISM is another one of those diseases for which it is said there is no cure. In my practice I have had much to do with patients thus afflicted, and I have not found it difficult to give relief in a short time.

By giving sudorific medicine to promote perspiration, and bathing the feet in tepid water with ashes added at night before retiring to bed, drinking freely of catnip or other herb tea, and applying stimulating liniment to the affected parts, relief is obtained by the sufferer.

Continue by covering up warm in the bed, and in the morning take a dose of physic before breakfast. After its operation, take tonic three or four times a day, and continue to apply the heating liniment to the painful parts, if there be no heating or swelling. But if there be inflammation and swelling, use a cooling liniment to the parts and give a dose of physic every day or every other day, according to circumstances. If restless at night, give an anodyne to promote sleep.

I am aware that application of bathing liniments is objected to by many as worthless, but in my experience I have found it accompanied with the happiest results. Let sceptics say what they may, it is nevertheless true that, by keeping up a determination to the surface, the stomach and bowels cleansed, and the system in tone by tonics, rheumatism can be cured.

I am sorry to say that most of those cures which are effected outside of the medical faculty are reproachfully spoken of by them, although they be performed by men of candor and honesty. They cry "quack," and teach their adherents that it is better to die soon by their treatment than to live long by that of one who has not been to college or won a diploma. As though the keys of knowledge were exclusively within university walls! As though nature had not written truth and science in every root of the forest and in every leaf that grows!

But man is prone to beguile and deceive all he can, and then boast or pride himself upon possession of some intrinsic knowledge which

only such as himself hold the keys to un-
lock.

I am happy to think of the great Giver of all
good gifts, who is able and willing to impart
knowledge to all his creatures, and who moves
in such mysterious way that none can hinder.

I often look back upon my boyhood, and see
myself thinking and studying to know something.
No one to pity or aid me, but many to cast re-
proaches with haughty frowns, and say, "Knowledge is not for such as you. Oh, no, our schools
are closed against you; our advantages are not
for you to share. It is enough that you be
'hewers of wood and drawers of water.'"

The glad day rolled around when I found myself happily situated in the practice of medicine,
no thanks to any one. To me it has been a
source of much pleasure to know that I have been
a benefactor to mankind. I have attended diseases of all kinds with the most happy results.

A gentleman living at Marlton, in Evesham
township, was afflicted with inflammation or erysipelas of the head and arm. After being
attended by his family doctor, without good
results, mortification set in. The old gentleman

was persuaded to send for me against his own inclination, for he believed that a black man could not know anything. His prejudice had nearly cost him his life.

I called at his house on a Sunday afternoon, and found him in great agony. Examining the parts affected, I applied a small portion of my cancer-remedy with the point of a knife. Made a poultice and applied it. Gave a dose of sudorific medicine for that night, and a dose of antibilious powders for the next morning, to be taken before breakfast. I told them to apply a fresh poultice in the morning, and I would call on Monday.

I was punctual in appointment, examined the parts, found mortification arrested, and the patient much better,—to the great surprise of his family and friends, and to the mortification of the family physician, who boasted a sheepskin and strutted like a peacock. This same learned practitioner had been an army-surgeon, and doubtless had helped to chop off limbs from maimed bodies of our brave boys in the war. Many, perchance, who would now be living had they been let alone.

I continued to attend the old gentleman, with the best results. When the doctor learned that

mortification had been arrested he made the remark that a white man's knife would be needed to
finish the job. Hearing of this, I said to my
patient, " Have patience for a time, and you shall
soon see what nature can do in the case. The
living flesh and the dead flesh cannot unite again,
and there must be separation of the living from
the dead, and life must gain the supremacy." So
it turned out. The finger came off at the joint,
and healed nicely, to the satisfaction of himself
and friends, and to the humiliation of the family
doctor. In all probability, if the doctor had
pursued his course, and treated the case to the
end, he might have had a large bill, and have collected it from the old gentleman's executors, and
he would never have known how much his estate
had to contribute to the doctor for his skill in
depriving him of one hand.

We will take a glance at the different treat-
ments in the above case. The doctor claimed
science, which he learned at school; I acknowledge that the path of learning I never tried. I
have only observed nature, in which I see far the
greatest display of wisdom, which, if we follow,
we shall never go astray. From nature we learn

what we are and what we ought to be. Thus
every object of nature can furnish hints for contemplation. When I reflect upon how little I
know and how much the doctor knew, I am
utterly astonished! He treated the case in a
scientific manner without success; I treated it
according to the laws of nature.

Had I been first called in the above case, and
found inflammation rising in the diseased part, I
should at once have set about to arrest it and to
prevent mortification from setting in. It is easier
to ward off a monster than to fight him on his
own vantage ground.

I used the elm-bark poultice with yeast, applied
tepid, which soon corrected the fetor of the parts
and assisted nature to separate the mortified from
the living flesh. I also administered tonics to
brace the system, and cathartics to carry off feculent matter from the internal organs. Gave sudor-
ifics occasionally to keep up a determination to
the surface, and recommended a wholesome regi-
men.

I know that it is customary to amputate a limb
in case of mortification, with what propriety I am
unable to determine, as it is easily arrested by

very simple means; and when it cannot be, I have no evidence that the knife could save the life of the patient.

I believe if a proper course of treatment will not cure, there exists a faulty state of the constitution or of the ulcer or wound itself; and should amputation be performed the stump will slough, or the patient will sink from irritation or the direct consequences of the operation.

It appears strange to me that surgeons should direct us to wait until mortification has stopped before amputation be performed. Although they direct the removal of a mortified limb, they also direct that it be not done until mortification is arrested or until a line of demarcation is formed or separation takes place between the living and the dead parts. I would like to know how this doctrine can be reconciled with reason, common sense, philosophy, or correct principles of surgery. It appears most absurd to me, however it may appear to others; and this inconsistency is strikingly exemplified in practice at the bedside of the patient.

In cases of mortification the affected parts should be bathed at least twice a day in weak lye, a little warm, for several minutes at a time, and poultice applied of yeast, charcoal, and elm-flour until all the mortified portions slough off. Then a healing salve applied till well. Purgatives being given throughout the affliction, and tonics also to keep up the strength.

CHAPTER XXV.

My practice in treating cancers has been large, and with many I have had the most satisfactory results, and have effected radical cures.

I consider cancers a disease of the very worst kind. They spread in a rapid manner, discharge a thin, acrimonious matter that excoriates the surrounding integuments, and emits a very fetid smell. They are mostly confined to the glandular parts, particularly the breast of the female; sometimes the face, the uterus, the lower lip, the eye, or tongue. They are generally met with in persons advanced in life. In women about the period that the menses terminate.

There are different species of this disease, some of which continue many years without much injury. Cancer of the female breast proceeds to a more speedy termination, hastened often from an operation by the knife. I have had much experience in them, both before and after cutting, and have found them the most distressing of diseases to which poor mortals are subject. The patient is literally destroyed by a slow and virulent poison, with which the fluids of the system are contaminated.

I am free to give my testimony against the use of the knife in any case whatever, for I am satisfied that it only aggravates the disease, and must shorten the life of the patient. It exasperates and accelerates the growth of the poisonous thing, and cannot possibly penetrate so far as the poison itself extends. Neither could the subject bear the operation of having the whole extirpated. If he could there might be some probability of thus effecting a cure, but the blood and mass of fluids in the system are in a greater or less degree contaminated, and it betrays consummate folly to employ the knife with the view of eradicating the disease.

It is evident that the constitution is more or less affected; and with what propriety or prospect of success can such cruel and unnatural means be relied on I am unable to say.

I have treated cancers in every stage of their growth, and though some were obstinate and incurable, I have had many good results. I think many more would have been cured, but it seems that persons afflicted with cancer become very irritable, and in a great measure lose that proper control of themselves that is necessary in all bad cases.

All afflicted persons have a great many friends and advisers who, as I have said before, are apt to do more harm than good. The patient is apt to listen with hope, and every one knows what is best to do and where to go to get cured, and they are apt to be led to destruction. In such cases, therefore, the best skill must fail. I do not know of any specifics, either for cancers or any diseases, but there are medicines which may be relied upon in a majority of cases, although much depends on the patient.

Some suppose they must be cured in a few days, and in that case they will change from one course of treatment to another. Others are led to believe that there is no cure, having been taught so by the doctors; therefore they will give all the trouble they can, and will not follow any directions. In such cases medicines are of little or no use. Others, again, have more work to do whilst afflicted, fearing that death may come before they get done, and these will do everything that they are forbidden to do.

There is now and then one that will say, " I came to get cured," and I have observed that such are very apt to become cured.

The patient needs to be quiet nervously, not overworked, mind and body in healthy action. I believe that I never had one who came to me in the earlier stages of the disease, saying, " I have come to obey you and to be cured," but that that one was cured.

" It was no cancer," say the faculty, " or it could not have been cured ; cure for that has never been discovered. Such practice is quackery."

This seems to me like a man being rescued from drowning by one who is not a waterman. The man who has fallen in the river looks and sees nothing but the near approach of death. Great is his excitement. He struggles, but cannot extricate himself. The watery element he cannot overcome. Providentially, some one arrives just in time to lend him a helping hand and assist him safely to land.

We imagine his exclamation, " Oh, happy

deliverance, I am saved!" He will not upbraid his deliverer for not being some great seaman or mariner. He will not question him of his knowledge of the compass, or of the sea, or of navigation. Oh, no, his friends, finding him saved, will not accuse him of being a fool, or rebuke him for inconsistency. They will not tell him that he should have sent for a great navigator to save him, and spurned the assistance of one unacquainted with the water.

Or, could one pass by and see a person struggling in the river for life without so much as throwing a board or something that he might grasp wherewith to assist himself and be saved from a watery grave?

Thus, by the just laws of nature we learn to do good. We feel it incumbent upon us to cultivate our faculties for the good of ourselves and fellow-men. We, who have not had equal advantages with the learned, must not sit down and fold our arms and say, "I know nothing, because no one has taught me," but we must study nature and its laws, from whence all mighty truths are drawn, by assiduously applying our minds to that which is good, trusting to the great Giver of all good gifts, whose wisdom is unsearchable, and His ways past finding out.

There is a thing which more than all others has been a source of much consolation to me, and that is God's justice to man. The noble and the ignoble alike have to pass through the gates of death to that spirit land where equality is the law. I hope no one will blame another for doing good to his fellow-man by extricating him from any trouble or affliction, whether it be from cancer or a watery grave.

It is not my purpose to write medical treatment of the various diseases, yet I cannot refrain from some remarks relative thereto, having spent much of my time in the practice of medicine and in the sick-room, and in the various forms of disease. I am astonished when I reflect upon the tardiness of the progress of learned men in knowledge of treatment of the sick, and the remedies most conducive to the health of the patient and least destructive to a healthy constitution.

I have long considered vegetable medicine all that is needed for the ills of the human family, and the most simple compounds the better. I know it is said that mercury or calomel is a necessary agent in arousing a torpid liver, and cannot well be dispensed with. I have no doubt that it will act upon the liver and all other organs, bones, muscles, constitution, and all, and bring on premature old age and death. In an experience of thirty-three years I have never given one grain of calomel under any circumstance. I have found the May-apple root, used as a purgative, to answer every purpose for which calomel is given, in acting on the liver by removing torpidity or any of the ailments for which calomel is given. At the same time, the patient will not be troubled with caries of the bones or incurable rheumatism; neither will he be a living barometer, to indicate the various changes of the weather. It seems to me that vegetable medicine is all that is needed for the restoration of health, the voice of the medical faculty to the contrary notwithstanding.

In the early part of my practice some people would say, "What does he know about medicine? he will poison you." They had no fears of the doctor who had been to college, and who was handling and dealing out the most deadly poisons to his patients every day. I suppose they thought if it was only sanctioned by educated men it would greatly modify the poison, or prove a complete antidote, not knowing that poison is poison by whosoever administered.

Persons little thought that in me was caution, and a love of truthfulness, and a particular regard for my fellow-men. It was a pleasant satisfaction to me to know that I was not duping my fellow-men, knowing that I was using the most harmless preparations.

I know there are a good many vegetables that are poison. Of these I make the least use, and have seldom found it necessary to use them at all except as external applications, and then with great caution, fearing they might be absorbed and taken into the circulation, and cause mischief to the patient. I am opposed to deadly poisons or the use of the knife. Each has had its votaries, notwithstanding, and each from some cause unknown has seemed to be a benefit, but the cases are rare.

A gentleman living near Bordentown, New Jersey, was afflicted with cancer of the delicate parts. He called upon me, not knowing what was the matter. On examination, I discovered it to be cancer, and stated the fact to him plainly. Of

course, he was anxious to know what chance
there was for a cure, and what it would cost him
to be cured. I told him that I thought it could
be cured, and that it would cost him twenty-five
dollars. He demurred, and thought five sufficient. It was a case which would require great
caution in treatment, and I was annoyed that he
should set so small an estimate upon his life.

I explained his condition to him fully, and told
him that eminent surgeons would charge him
hundreds or thousands of dollars, and that perhaps
it would cost him his life in the end. I think he
called on me three times with the remark that he
thought he was better but that I had not yet cured
him. I thought he was getting restless, and my
feelings were that he intended to go somewhere
else for treatment. I had no objections, of course,
except that my judgment was to the effect that
for his own good he better continue as he had
begun. He left me, however, and I have learned
since that he had an operation performed, and that
he is living with no hope of being cured, and that
he is a great sufferer.

Right sorry am I that his prejudice, together
with his opaque mind, should lead him to de-

struction. I heard that some one of his near relatives denounced me for speaking so plain; I hope they have had time to consider that the truth of what I said to them is being verified. He is living without the hope of ever spending another happy or peaceful day with his family and friends; suffering, if possible, the pains of ten thousand deaths, from which he cannot extricate himself. Beside, the stench emitted from him makes him very unpleasant company even to his companion and dearest friends. Ere long his wife shall be a widow and his children fatherless. He was just in the flower of his age and the vigor of his youth, when the world was looking to him as a happy home.

Ambition prompted him to have an operation performed against the admonition of one who has a love for mankind, and the once happy home and fireside, where all was pleasure and luxury, is now desolate. It is a solemn thing for loved ones to be separated by death, but by proper preparation they will meet again in the Elysian fields, to part no more.

There is one thing I wish to remark, and that is how little we know of ourselves, and how we are carried away by the opinions of others. We know nothing of what is best for ourselves, particularly in medicine. We are apt to found our beliefs on the many beliefs of others which look to us so plausible. We adapt these things to our notions without just consideration, which envelops us in the most pitiable mental darkness.

We are told there is none who can treat our ills or administer medicine with the same promptness as the regular graduate, all of which is very plausible. Such should be the foundation for us to build upon should there be truth and justice enough to rivet such assurances. Others claim the Indian knows more about the healing art than all others; by what right I am not able to say, for certainly they are said to be the most stupid and ignorant of all people. I have but little faith in such superstitious people. Some claim that by natural instinct the Indian is a doctor, which seems to me quite a rebuke to the medical faculty, seeming to assert that natural knowledge is quite superior to any other; superior to the knowledge of men who have spent gold by thousands and roamed over foreign lands to read mankind, their laws, their arts, " Who have old Greece and Rome surveyed, and the vast sense of Plato weighed," all for knowledge. There is mystery somewhere; that we must leave for the reader to solve.

Again, we see some educated men practising what they call "Indian Remedies," as pills, bitters, and cough syrups. They are quite sure to realize a fortune by using the Indians' name, at the same time they know well that this same remedy is their own invention, with the name of Indian added as an adjuvant, as a ruse to assist its sale. While the vender reaps a fortune, few doubt his remedies, and thousands patronize without investigation.

It has often seemed strange to me that persons will study interests in lands, stocks, financial and commercial; study how to accumulate wealth, how to make good bargains in their own favor, and how to prevent themselves from being imposed upon, and yet neglect the study of health and longevity, two of the most important things in an earthly career. Health is a greater boon than riches, surpassing every earthly blessing.

Taking a general survey of mankind, I find them of all conditions in life. Some reared in penury and ignorance, deprived of the blessings of an education, no one to tutor or to cultivate; having been born in smoky hovels, where nothing was to be learned but debauchery and profanity; clad and fed roughly, hardened in look and gesture, uncleanly in habits, and morals bad. These are looked upon by the more favored classes as little above the beasts, are shunned, and are not admitted into the association of the higher classes.

What a deplorable condition! In their poverty they have but few friends; in sickness their neighbors pay a cold respect; in death there are but few to mourn their loss and attend them to the tomb. There is no eulogium delivered on the occasion; some one may venture to offer the coldest of prayers. Perhaps it is only for formality, for it seems to be without spirit. I have often thought the ministers of the gospel were much to blame for this ignorant class of people. Christ came poor and to the poor. The example is a good one and worthy to be followed.

The poor man's memory is soon blotted out, to be remembered no more. If he had died rich, his cold remains would have drawn a great concourse of people to his funeral. There would have been anxious inquiries about his wealth,—who was to have it, and how he got it.

We will now contrast the great and rich man with the poor one. He was born in opulence, nurtured till manhood. Every avenue is open before him. His tutors are the best that can be selected. He enjoys the company of the wise and great. He is sent to foreign lands to learn their manners and customs. He is clothed in purple and fine linen, knows no wants, feeds on the richest viands, his boots are not besmeared with the mud of the field. He looks upon manual labor as the business for other hands, and not his. In the heat of summer he reposes in the shade; in the cold of winter has his comfortable abode. He is surrounded with all the luxuries of life, with nothing to disturb his mind.

He reads law, medicine, gospel, and the popular sciences. Makes choice of a profession that he thinks most popular, or from which he will derive the most honor, financially and politically. He enters the arena of life bold and defiant, and is made official of State and nation. He prides himself upon his dignity, and is a mighty combatant in any and every place where his profession calls him. He claims the leadership of his colleagues; aspires to greatness. His opponents dread him, for he will not be talked down, even when in the wrong. He uses his tongue as the master does his lash, to inflict terror on all around him, fighting for laurels with which he hopes to be crowned.

Finally he imbibes his wine to give animation to torpitude, and to confirm his vociferations he mixes profanity with his language. He sneers at the more humble portion of mankind, and by looks and gestures seems to think them of inferior material to himself. He never complains of his salary being too high, but often complains of the poor man's hire. Writing and delivering many lectures in the halls of the State and nation, his literature is strewn broadcast over the land. His vulpine ways are not visible to all; he is looking forward to the goose that lays the golden egg. Lauded to the skies by newspapers which are in favor of him, while others criticise, he comes to the conclusion that he is worthy of the highest place in the gift of the people, for which some have leaped and, missing the rock, have passed over into the abyss on the other side and sunk to rise no more, never to be found by the best grappling irons, or if by good fortune they escaped, hastened into retirement, not to live long to plague any one.

Also missing his aim, our hero's mind, in the cool shades of retirement, reverts to the past to wonder why this disappointment should be his. Unsatisfied ambition and luxurious living begin to tell heavily upon him. He has lost that vividness that was once manifest in all those great halls, which then were heaven enough for him, and like Lucifer has fallen to rise no more; yet he leans to his favorite calling.

Finally he is summoned to appear before his God, which summons he must obey without demur. His cherished tactics are of no avail before the Judge; he must haste away to a world where all are equal according to their deeds. He yieldeth up the ghost and is no more.

Thousands speak of him as a loss to the State; national flags all over the country are thrown at half-mast. Rich and poor alike mourn for him. He is placed in state where all can look upon him. A great man has died. Cannon are fired. He is eulogized to the skies,—it is almost impossible to find language to utter his praise. His good deeds are spoken of, but his bad ones never. Some will speak of his death as though he were eternal and could not die. Monuments are erected to his memory and mark his last resting-place, and point out to the traveller from foreign lands that a great man lies there. His widow and children are consoled by resolutions of respect; every provision is made to make them happy, and to save them from want financially. The poor and the rich sympathize, and expressions of sorrow are visible on all who exclaim,—

> Here a man of state hath fallen,—
> Stop and shed a tear or two;
> Who will fill his able calling?
> Few are left that are able to.
>
> Like a lion fierce and mighty,
> The small and humble crouch to see him;
> His voice like thunder was terrific,
> When on the stand or in the pulpit.

CHAPTER XXVI.

In the year eighteen hundred and seventy-five, as my health seemed to be improving slowly, I proposed to build a barn, and commenced to make the necessary preparations. Feeling so much better than I had for the last year or two, I did not think the excitement would be such as to cause a relapse. In a little time, however, I found myself retrograding. My office practice was large, having several cancer cases that were obstinate, and although I did not feel well, I knew no other way than to fight out my duties upon the line on which I had begun them.

The barn was thirty by thirty-two feet, with wagon-house at one end, and corn-crib therein, cow-house at the other, with overshot; all at a cost of about ten or twelve hundred dollars. I was glad when the building was finished, for I could once more resume my office-duties without interruption, and devote my whole attention to them.

The summer of eighteen hundred and seventy-five was an eventful one. Being extremely dry weather, the wells failed throughout all sections of the country. East, west, north, and south persons became alarmed, as the oldest inhabitant could remember no such drought for fifty years.

Corn, notwithstanding, grew well and produced heavily. The early potato crop yielded well, but the later crop was destroyed by a kind of bug that was new to us, unknown before in this section of country. Various means were used to prevent the entire crop from being destroyed; poisons were sprinkled on the vines without the desired results. Some farmers hand picked the bugs by barrels and burned them, but in a few days the insects returned as numerous as ever. Whence they came was a mystery. If the vines were all freed from them on one day, they seemed to come again on the next day in as great numbers as before. The hay crop also failed.

The dried-up wells, the failure of crops in hay and potatoes, made quite a prospect of famine, from which, under a gracious Providence, we were happily saved.

Besides this, many of the largest city firms and

richest men failed, and thousands of laborers were thrown out of employment. These flooded city and country,—in companies of eight and ten passing through the land,—so that many inhabitants of the country became alarmed for the safety of person and property.

The winter previous had been a hard one, long and cold,—so severe that it seemed to kill the frogs and mice and moles, also many roots of vegetables in the ground. When the spring came it seemed strange not to hear the croaking of frogs as usual.

Notwithstanding the hard times, there was not so much pillaging by the poor as was anticipated. There were heavy burglaries committed in various parts of the country, it is true, such as bank robberies, and heavy defalcations, but this was done by professionals who knew how to appreciate large sums of money. There were also many murders in this year. To a great degree men were demoralized and demoniacal, bent upon revenging the most trivial insult, and not hesitating for a moment to use the pistol and the knife. The law, also, was so entangled that it seemed difficult to reach extremely bad cases. Able lawyers screened murder cases under a plea of insanity, and the guilty were permitted to go free. Money and wealth, too, seemed to hide iniquity. Some of the most eminent clergymen in the country were before the courts for crimes alleged against them. Landed property became low, money scarce, and business depressed. Many suicides were committed on account of destitution or fear of want.

The time to economize had fully come, but those who had been living luxuriously found retrenchment difficult. When nature is in commotion, all other things sympathize more or less. Perhaps man's corrupt, unlimited will has provoked the commotion of nature for chastisement, to which if we take heed we shall do well.

It seems to me that pride was the one great cause which brought such hard times upon us. Had we lived a little more frugal whilst in our prosperity, whilst money was plenty, 'twas then we should have curbed our lusts for that which we were not able to carry to the end. It was then we should have laid by some of our earnings for an unforeseen stormy day. Fashion was the destroyer of all our happiness, and we were bound to keep pace with our neighbor, and endeavor to surpass him in dress or ornaments of the house, or in travelling on cars from place to place, spending hard-earned money for no equivalent.

Most all seemed willing and ready and anxious to spend the last dollar for some gaudy dress either for the head, back, or feet, forgetting at the same time the required quantity, double or treble, what it used to be in their grandfather's or grandmother's time. They were not looking forward to a rainy or sick day. Suspension was not in the count. They never consulted the economy of the ant or the bee, to see how diligently they worked in summer to lay up for the winter.

I believe that most people may be in better circumstances if they would only be frugal in dealing; make it a point to lay by some portion of their earnings every day or week, and resolve that it is better to be poor while young than poor in old age. By a strict adherence to economy, and promptly abstaining from frivolous notions, any one will become rich.

Riches are gained more by saving than by earning. It is no matter how much one earns; he can spend it all in less time than it took to earn it, and still be poor. A man who is saving is often called mean and stingy; no doubt some are so, but I have often thought if it were not for some saving, there would be none to help another.

It seems to me this class is a necessary blessing. They are in a great measure guardians for the spendthrift, who knows no want until he becomes involved in ruin. They are the garner or storehouse where the harvest is laid up for a time of need. Indeed, here we see that abstemiousness and frugality are the prolific means by which men become rich and happy.

The fall of eighteen hundred and seventy-five was mild and warm, as was also the early winter. One cold snap in December made ice some five inches thick, and many availed themselves of this opportunity to fill their ice-houses. These were wise, for no cold so severe occurred again during the season. There were not many heavy rains, but cloudy weather and high winds alternated until the last of January, eighteen hundred and seventy-six.

About the fifteenth of January, of this year, we had a cold spell of a few days, which made ice some three inches thick, and many made the best use of the occasion to collect all they could, thinking that thin ice would be better than none.

The ground was bare, not enough snow had at any one time fallen to cover it, neither was it frozen to any depth.

How it will be from this until the first of May, when the Centennial Exhibition opens, remains to be seen; at the near approach of this many people are rejoicing, hoping that times will change for the better and remove that lamentable depression which has so long been resting upon them like an incubus. I am inclined to think that the spring will bring with it rejoicing and gladness to all hearts and homes, and plenty supply the place of want, and cheerfulness chase gloom away to where the human family does not dwell.

I have a sister who, while living in Philadelphia, some time ago unfortunately became blind with cataract. She applied to one of the most noted physicians there, who performed an operation, but without good result. Learning of her condition, I hastened to see her, and was determined that a physician of celebrity, of whom I had heard through a friend (who in case of cataract had had vision partially restored), and of whom I had a high opinion, should pass judgment upon her.

I procured his card, took my sister to the office, and had an interview with him relative to her case. I told him that the woman was poor, that she had not one dollar to pay for the operation, but that she was anxious to be restored to sight, and that the charge I myself would pay, hoping he would be successful.

He then made an examination, and said that the condition of the eyes was such that he could give her one good eye. "What will you charge her?" I asked. "Two hundred dollars." At this I hesitated, for it seemed a high rate. He appeared to doubt my authenticalness, and I gave him the names of neighbors to whom he could refer, if he wished, for the truth of my expression. I told him that I hoped he would be successful, and that he also would be as moderate in charge as possible.

He assured me that he would restore one eye, and that two hundred dollars was one hundred less than his usual charge. He mentioned several cases in the infirmaries and in private residences where he had operated, and never in a single instance failed. "I trust this will not be your first failure," I said.

The trial to my sister, however, proved fruitless. I paid the money, which he accepted without a murmur, and during the two full years since my sister has not seen the light of the sun. He has his money, and my sister has her blindness. Why the doctor in this case did not succeed, I am unable to say. It seems to me it would have been but fair not to have claimed the full charge, in that no good was done; but we must be content to be duped by such men from the temples of education, who can chat like magpies, whose skill is in the tongue and not in the head. Great is the pity that truth and justice are so far below par with the so-called wise and good, when they should be the leading lights of the world.

I have referred to the above case to show that the most learned and skilled in the medical profession make woful blunders in their practice, and receive therefor large remunerations, and are lauded to the skies for the knowledge they obtain from some seminary, whose intellectual training never dare be disputed by the so-called illiterate.

Strange though it may appear to others, it seems to me that truth and justice are the principles by which we should work our way through

life.   In all our dealings let truth be our guiding-
star, which, if we keep in view, we shall not go
astray, and our way will be lit up with justice to
all men, a diadem of beauty on our heads.   We
shall not then have fear of each other, but all the
paths shall be peace and safety throughout our
broad land.   Covetousness shall be dispelled from
every breast, and joy and happiness predominate.

CHAPTER XXVII.

It has long been my opinion that the colored people as a race have much to blame in themselves for their present condition.

True, we have been in bondage all or most of our lives, and thus shut out from advantages social and educational. Of the few who were redeemed years ago by great labor and personal sacrifice, and sometimes at the cost of human life, only a part of them appreciate their altered condition. Some have made their freedom a by-word and a jest.

The race is too much addicted to indolence and self-pride. Each would like to be the leader or orator of the race. They would like to occupy positions of ease, but are unwilling to pursue the path of labor, which only brings peace, and comfort, and success. They are too much delighted with parties, festivals, and all places of amusement, from which they reap no reward.

The husbands love personal comfort, and are outraged if wives are not general attendants at washing-places during the week. They think it too much to maintain a wife at home, or to hold sacred any obligation to children, and hold that they can break the conjugal or parental relation at will.

Many of these are church members, and seemingly happy in their way of devotion. They hold long meetings, make long prayers, and use odd gestures, enter the meeting at any time during service, and also go out at will. Christ denounced such worship as this, as did he also inculcate truth. Punctuality is a part of sincere worship, yet this is a great fault among colored people. The hour appointed for worship is the hour to be there, but they manifest great carelessness with regard to their word, and continue to come in from the beginning to the end of the meeting. Perhaps they will be accountable for untruthfulness.

There is also much said by our people about the prejudice between the two races. I admit there is too much; but how can it be otherwise than manifested when a white and colored man meet each other and both are full of prejudice against each other? Therefore it is hard to tell which has the most. But when white and colored Christians meet in the true freedom of their Lord there is no prejudice, for all things have become new.

My colored friends, should you conduct yourselves on true moral principles, not gaudy in manners nor boisterous in talk, your ways calm and decisive, your word so sacred that 'tis never violated, your promises fulfilled, your debts paid, modest in all things and meddlesome in none, you shall find the monster Prejudice only a thing to be talked about. Merit alone will promote you to respect. You will also see the prejudice between the whites of the higher and lower classes. It is not expected that the rich and refined should mingle with the poor and low. It is no matter what color they are, my experience for the last thirty years is that man is man according to merit. Where truth and prosperity are in the ascending, prejudice is in the descending, scale. Many a colored man supposes, and so does many a white one, that when he is making money his neighbors will estimate him by the show he makes. He does not seem to understand that humility should dwell with frailty, and atone for ignorance, error, and imperfection. In all my practice I have ever found that prejudice would skulk when confronted by common sense. I cannot see but that I have had a full share of practice. I have been treated with all due respect. Every color and class has its preferences, for reasons inherent in one's very being; to account for certain predilections would be simply impossible.

Thus we see also among the learned and great men as a proof, say, there is to be a man elected to some high office of the State or nation. He is not run singly, but with opposition. Two are nominated, all things considered, of equal ability. Their propensities for good or bad are proclaimed aloud. Persons are prejudiced on both sides. Some choose one and some the other, and the two parties become regular combatants. Money on each side is freely lavished, even though those who lavish it will only be the losers. Here we see prejudice in its might with no good reason therefor. One or the other must win the race. There is a prejudice used for an accommodation between white and colored people ; for instance, a white and a colored person are ever so familiar for a long time, they eat and drink with each other, they share each other's pleasures, what belongs to one is common stock to both, they could not enjoy each other more were they of the same color.

Peradventure, each one's business calls him from home to the same place. Then they meet numerous people from different sections. The white and the colored meet each other. They are not the same jovial friends that they were at home. The white man will give his colored friend an askance look by way of recognition and to show the company that he holds himself higher than a colored man. They both feel the sting, but this is prejudice for accommodation.

Perhaps we, the colored people, are somewhat to blame for this treatment. Let us ask ourselves why it is so. The answer is, we are not possessors of lands and stocks, etc. We have been content to be waiters and coachmen, and would be happy to sit down in our leisure moments and tell about the fine coach and horses committed to our charge. This we could do with considerable flourish, and with as much pride as though they were ours. This did not require much manual labor, of which we never were fond.

Cities have been the places of our choice. It is dignifying to be called a citizen, and sight-seeing was a great thing to us. Besides, if a man lived in the country and labored in the fields, he was not considered sane, even though he possessed more than twenty citizens of the colored race. I am sorry that this state of things exists. It is nevertheless true, and all complain of prejudice and hard times. It is what they have worked for, and they are now receiving their pay, richly but reluctantly.

To every colored man who wishes to rise, to kill a prejudice that rests in his path, I say leave the city and go to the country, where land is cheap; purchase what you can and go to work; raise your own bread and butter; be frugal; bring up your children yourselves, and teach them to labor; teach them that the farmer holds the keys of the storehouses of the nations. Through them comes the staff of life; through them merchants live and indolent gentlemen loll at jovial boards. Men of equal ability are just

the same as two ten-pound weights; one placed
in a balance cannot weigh the other down, as
there will be no choice, for there will be ten
pounds on each side. It is ten pounds and no
more.

As I write, a colored man steps into my office.
After the common salutation, I remark, "I have
not seen you for a long time; where have you
been?" "Well, I was at a watering-place all summer, and after that went to wait upon a doctor."
"Were wages good?" I asked. "No; nothing."
"You did not work for nothing, did you?" "As
good as nothing," he replied; "only twelve dollars
per month." "But that is better than nothing;
your work was not heavy and your board was in-
cluded."

"Oh, I had rather beg than work at that price!"
he said. "My wife was there too, and she got only
two dollars per week."

"You must consider that these are hard times,"
I argued. "If you and your wife had continued for
four months you would have had eighty dollars
coming to you, beside your board, fuel, and rent.
I consider that would have been quite an item in
these times."

" Oh, there's plenty of money in the country, but they do not want to pay a man for his labor."

" Well, I admit there is plenty of money in the hands of those who have saved it, but there is nothing doing to cause it to circulate. When I was a young man, we thought eight or ten dollars a month good wages for men, and seventy-five cents a week good wages for women, and all seemed satisfied."

" Yes, but everything was lower then," he continued.

" Yes," said I, " and persons not so vain and foolish. I think the colored people much at fault for living as they do. If they would leave the towns and move into the forest, where land is cheap, buy, and go to work and raise their living and become land-holders, how much better it would show for them."

He admitted this, but added that the wives of colored men were too proud for that.

I then told him of a man who came from the old country, who told me that on arriving at Burlington, New Jersey, he had but six cents, and that he gave for a glass of whiskey, and that he knew another who had done the same thing, and was now owner of two or three farms.

"I am sorry," I said, "that the colored people want their good things as they go along, and rags and poverty in their old age. As to begging or stealing, I should be ashamed. I do not think there is much honor in either, even in old age, if one has had his health in his young days."

I have always been opposed to separate colored churches and schools, for several reasons. "God is love," and we are commanded to love one another, "not as Cain, who was of the wicked one." Also, "Whosoever hateth his brother is a murderer." Further, "Beloved, let us love one another, for love is of God." "If God so loved us, we ought also to love one another." "He that dwelleth in love, dwelleth in God and God in him." "There is no fear in love, but perfect love casteth out fear, because fear hath torment." "He that feareth is not made perfect in love." "Whosoever believeth that Jesus is the Christ is born of God, and every one that loveth Him that begat, loveth Him also that is begotten of Him."

I am not able to understand how we are to be the possessors of these beatifical blessings, and at

the same time entertain in our hearts a malignity
which forbids us to worship together the Holy
God of love. I have always believed the separation of the churches a trick of the devil to keep
open the chasm between Christians, into which I
fear many shall fall and be lost to all eternity. I
believe Christianity would have been far advanced
to-day had not the churches separated. When
an army goes into the field to fight its enemy it
were best to confront it with a whole army, and
confide for succor in the chief commander, God. I
do not think that it was intended by the Almighty
that separate worship and separate heavens were
for the different colors of mankind. Unity of worship would have promoted morality, sociableness,
and helped to break down the middle wall of
existing prejudice. It would clearly have demon-
strated to the world that we were sons of God,
because we lived together in love.

I think it would have been an advantage to my
own race, by making us more guarded in expression, and saved us from the ridicule which sometimes we receive justly for eccentricities in worship.
I have myself been caused to laugh at the sermons
delivered by colored preachers; at the same time,

they were a shame to the Christianity in both the white and the colored races.

But some of my colored friends will say, " If we had not withdrawn from the white congregations we would have had no liberties in the church, we could not have become preachers and leaders." To any friend who may entertain this sentiment, I say, " If you were called of God to preach or to lead, if God had a message to deliver to the world through you, not all the powers of darkness could have prevailed against you." " If God be for us, who shall be against us?" He is more than all that could be against us. " But we have to take back seats," one says. If you are one of God's soldiers one would be able to chase a thousand, and two to put ten thousand to flight. " When we get happy, we cannot shout," some one else will say; "the white members look upon us frowningly." Perhaps the white brethren are like myself, in that I was looking to see their light shining daily. They look for truth, continency, love of virtue, all of which if we practise we shall do well.

I think every person should read Christ's Sermon on the Mount for instruction. There the Lord says that we should not be as the hypo-

crites, who love to pray standing in the syna-
gogues and in the corners of the streets that they
may be seen of men, but He recommends closet
prayer as that which shall bring the open reward.
And says again, that except your righteousness
shall exceed the righteousness of the scribes and
Pharisees, ye shall in no case enter into the kingdom of heaven.

I do not know from whom we could have received better instruction. Again, by separation
we become strangers to each other, white and
colored, and when we meet it is in that inimical
manner in which we are more like heathens than
like Christian friends, thus making the moments
when we are together tedious and barren. This
exhibition is at once a strong blow against Christianity before a sinful world of mankind.

I have been opposed to colored schools wholly
because they were against the principles of Christian fellowship. I think that co-education would
be beneficial to each race. First, it would establish
Christian unity. It would elevate the colored race
by a sort of refinement in their expression. It
would make them believe that they were a part
and parcel of mankind. It would arouse in them

the desire to be cleanly and as refined as their class-mates. It would stimulate them to love education, and to appreciate it. It would dispel that horrible idea that they were esteemed nothing above the beast. It would make them feel justice to be a reality and not a sham.

Separate schools are debasing to the manners of each, whilst it causes the one to imbibe imbecility and the other superiority, thus fixing a great gulf between them, which shall be impassable. It plants the seed of hate in their youthful hearts, and there it is watered from the streams of strife until it becomes so deeply rooted that it grows to a large tree, whose branches spread over the whole land and become the habitation of every unclean and hateful bird, and its fruit is poisonous to the nation. Separation causes in the colored child hate, and unbecoming behavior, and habitual idleness with indelible slovenliness; for all of which, I fear, a Christian republic will have to render an account.

I have sometimes thought it strange that Christians in our enlightened land manifest such zeal for the poor heathen of other lands as to send ministers and money for their civilization, when at

their own doors thousands are compelled to wal-
low all their days, from the cradle to the grave,
among the most dispiteous of mankind, and are
the recipients of cold rebuke from those they have
known all their lives. I can only say, with Jeffer-
son, that I tremble for my country when I reflect
that God is just, and that his justice cannot sleep
forever.

It seems to me that unity and hate are a part of
Christian civilization, because it is taught to the
little children in the schools that to do justice and
righteousness to the colored children is a flagrant
wrong. Thus it becomes a part of their early
education. I am sorry to say that such are the
facts with few exceptions, and the more the shame
to Christendom.

In my own experience I can bear testimony to
the good results arising from the unity of schools.
Fortunately for me I never attended any but a
white school, and that but little. We shared each
other's sports and pleasures to a great extent, and
we imbibed a sympathy which time has never
obliterated, and since we have arrived at manhood
and womanhood we seldom or never meet but
that our young school days are referred to, and

we greet each other as old friends and not as
heathen enemies. They frequently make their
boast when we meet in company that we are old
school-mates. They assert that we played together, read in class together, and wrestled together. Indeed, they seem proud to recognize me
as one of them; whereas, if we had been in separate schools, how different would our greeting be!
In this we see harmony exemplified. Or should
we have relatives settled in foreign parts, and one
of those school-mates should happen to travel
that way and hear the name mentioned, I have
known him to travel quite out of the way to see a
brother or sister of his old colored school-mate,
and make himself known by saying, "I used to
go to school with your brother or sister," as the
case might be, and have a happy greeting.

No long since a gentleman called at my office
and, saluting me, said, "I don't think you recognize
me." After a moment's hesitation I said, "I do
not seem to recollect you." "Do you not remember attending my father at a certain time and
place?" he asked. "Oh, yes." "Well," he replied, "I am such a son of his, and used to know
you well; but I have been away for several years,

and being at present a few miles from here I could not go away without seeing you. I am now living in Florida, and I found one of your sisters there, and went to see her, and had quite a chat with her, and was glad to meet an old acquaintance of my father out there; and I tell you your sister is doing well out there, and when I return I will tell her I paid you a flying visit."

I thanked him for his favor, and we congratulated each other on our present and future prospect, both temporal and spiritual, hoping, at the same time, that if we should not meet again in this low ground of sorrow, we would meet on the Elysian fields, where our love would be reciprocal.

Many other pleasant incidents have arisen out of my early school associations. Persons have come to my office and introduced themselves by saying, "I am such an one's child. My father or mother used to go to school with you when you were young." They actually seemed to claim a right to be sociable, and I would quite put myself to trouble to inquire after the parents, and where they lived, and of their health and well-doing.

Often they would remark, "My parents would

be glad to see you; I have often heard them speak of you." All of which I consider was brought about by unity in school. We imbibed thus early a respect for each other which time has not obliterated.

Not long since a gentleman from Bristol, Pennsylvania, came into my office, and, after the common greeting, said, "My wife used to go to school with you." He being a stranger to me, I asked where, and what was her name. I was much surprised at his reply, and, sitting down, I exclaimed, "That is over fifty years ago, and I have often asked about that family and could learn nothing of them. Now," I said, "do tell me what ever became of a certain brother of your wife?" "Oh," he answered, "he died many years ago, and they all are dead except my wife, and she would like to see you very much."

"Tell her," I said, "to come and see me. I shall be pleased to see her." Although we were strangers to each other, we talked half a day about many things that had transpired at the old schoolhouse where his wife and I were children together. I related to him the circumstance of his wife's father being drowned when we were children, and he refreshed my memory in many things from what he had heard her say.

Thus, after an elapse of more than fifty years, these first principles of friendship were not destroyed, and we congratulated ourselves upon the fact that we were still living and could hear of each other once more in our old age.

I fear the day is far distant when Christianity and civilization shall predominate throughout our broad land. It seems to me to be the name, instead of the rule, that guides us. When I reflect for a moment I am constrained to fear that there are few that shall be saved, although we boast of a land of Bibles, a land of churches, a land of Christian light and liberty, where there are none to molest or to make us afraid. I fear that the heathen will go into the kingdom of heaven before us.

Our children may rise up in another generation to condemn us, claiming that they lived as they were trained, that revenge and hate were instilled in their tender minds, grown with their growth, and strengthened with their strength. In the last great day who shall be able to evade the All-Seeing Eye that beholds the universe and its inhabitants at a glance? Perhaps then it will be too late to amend; sighs and tears will avail nothing, a dark and unhappy future must be the abode. The Elysium that was once accessible and intended for a future home is closed forever, and the pride and prejudice once exulted in has brought abasement. There will be no distinction in that day between the rich and the poor, the black or the white. All shall reap the reward of their doings, and there shall be unity of punishment without redress.

Clayton Wilkins, a life-long acquaintance, and brother of Amos, with whom I served my time, died February fifth, eighteen hundred and seventy-six. It seems proper that I should give him notice here, for he was well known throughout the country, and my own boyish associations were with the family.

He was born in Fostertown in seventeen hundred and ninety-five. His occupation was working at farm labor as a hired man. He never married and never kept house. To a small legacy left him from his father's estate he continued to add until he became quite wealthy. During the last years of his life, when health and strength began to fail, he quietly laid aside the implements of husbandry and lived among his relations, sometimes one and sometimes another, as long as he felt pleased to stay. The last four years of his life he spent with his niece, Rachel Wilkins, who also was living a single life, and owned a farm adjoining the father's estate, where Clayton was born. It seemed strange that he should be taken out of the world within two hundred yards of the place where he had first seen the light.

He lived rather an eccentric life, was not fond of pomp or show, was abstemious in his habits, never meddled with other people's business. He was uneducated, and compelled to trust to others to keep his accounts, notwithstanding he became rich, and left his wealth by will to his relations. He never was attached to any religious sect or denomination. For several years before his death he seemed to be in consumptive decline, and at last age and disease combined to overcome his stalwart form, and compelled him to yield to death, the king of terrors. A large concourse of friends and relatives followed him to his last resting place at Medford, where his parents had been laid before him.

Previous to Clayton Wilkins's death, my brother Samuel, the oldest living brother, passed away on the twenty-eighth of April, eighteen hundred and seventy-five. He, like many others, had seen many ups and downs, both spiritual and temporal. By industry and frugality he accumulated a competence sufficient to sustain him in his old age. His occupation was farming, in which he was an adept. He became the owner of a farm of one hundred and fifty acres, with stock and farming utensils sufficient for any emergency, thus making his last days very comfortable in the necessaries of life. He raised a family of seven children to be men and women. His wife preceded him by some eight years to the spirit land. During the rest of his life he remained a widower. He gave much time to reading the Bible, and was always delighted to quote from it in argument. He claimed to have confidence in God, his Saviour, for many years. When inflammation of the bladder, cystitis, attacked him, so rapid was its progress (nothing could be done to alleviate him) that in ten days his sufferings were relieved by death, and we hope that his pain and sufferings were changed to joy and happiness. He was born February twenty-sixth, eighteen hundred and seven, and died April twenty-eighth, eighteen hundred and seventy-five, aged sixty-eight years, two months, and two days.

CHAPTER XXVIII.

In the year of eighteen hundred and seventy-six, the Centennial year, I proposed to give some time to visiting the exhibition.

As I had been a long time reading of old countries, and their people, and their wares, and as I had travelled but little, being limited in time and means, I had to content myself as best I could. "Now," thought I, "the whole world is about to congregate, and I certainly will embrace the opportunity to attend the great Centennial."

The day of the opening arrived on May tenth, and, as I supposed the rush would be heavy on that day, I omitted to go, but on the next Friday week after the tenth I commenced.

Having solicited Dr. Rosell to accompany me, we met on the day appointed, and went. We passed in through the Main Building entrance, fee being fifty cents. We had not been in five minutes before I remarked to the doctor, "I have got my money's worth, and all I get after this will be clear gain." We travelled for some time in the Main Building, and it reminded me of the Queen of Sheba when she came from the uttermost parts of the earth to see the wisdom of Solomon, and she exclaimed, "Behold, the half was not told me."

I was completely astonished; I could but remark to the doctor, "The sight is magnificent in the extreme, but we can't see all the things." He wanted to know why. "Because," said I, "it is too much; but," I added, "now let us take a look through Orange Free State, to see if anything is doing there." There we beheld many splendid articles of manufacture. I observed their harness, which was very good. In taxidermy they seemed to be proficient, having some of the most splendid specimens I ever saw of various birds, I think, from the ostrich to the humming-bird. The ostrich eggs, and skins of various animals, also dried fruits, minerals, and cereals of many kinds. This constrained me to believe that somebody lived in Africa.

We passed into the Chinese department, where one may have thought, according to the appear-

ance of the people, that we should have little to
see. After viewing their crockery, or chinaware,
in this we were much mistaken. Their carving
was wonderful indeed. I saw a bedstead that was
twenty years in making, five men working at it
the whole time. I think the price they held it at
was five thousand dollars, which seemed to me a
very great price for a bedstead. But suppose that
it had been manufactured in this country with the
same number of men, and the same time spent
upon it, it would be valued at more than one
hundred and fifty thousand dollars.

Their exhibits were wonderful to me. Everything they had made a better appearance than the
clothes they wear. Indeed, their fabrics were of
fine silk, but made up in very odd style. I do
not know that I saw a lady among them. The
men wore their hair long and plaited, hanging
down the back to the waist, and some even farther
than that. The Japanese, too, had some wonderful exhibits, such as bedsteads, lanterns, and a
thousand other things that I cannot name. They,
too, are an odd-looking people, whose articles
exhibited were far better-looking than themselves.

In the Swedish department were some of the

most remarkable statues I ever saw. At first sight I mistook them for persons standing in a group. I drew near to see the chest move by respiration, but as I failed to detect that, not being satisfied, I looked them steadfastly in the eyes, and, finding those organs immovable, concluded they must be statues.

It was quite amusing to me to see many other persons in the same uncertain judgment with myself in this department. There were other wonderful exhibits, which I cannot name. We passed pretty well through the Main Building, glancing at the wonderful works of art, and it reminded me of the old lady I once read of who went out to see the cars running on the railroad for the first time in her life. Gazing at them with amazement, she exclaimed, " The wisdom of the Almighty is great, but oh, the invention of man !"

As this was a big thing, we had to keep moving on. In the Swiss department we saw the smallest watch in the world. It was not so large as a gold dollar, and was valued, I think, at nine hundred dollars.

I said to the doctor that if any one should steal that watch, and the police should be in pursuit, it would not be much trouble to swallow it, neither would it distend the stomach.

We also saw the large cake of silver that weighed four hundred and some odd pounds (I do not now distinctly recollect), valued at seventy-two thousand dollars. We also saw great quantities of gold and silver ore from the various parts of the world. I remarked to some one, "We have plenty of those kind of stones with us, but do not pretend to pick them up." The doctor laughed and seemed to think, "You Jerseymen are not very poor."

We saw the statues representing Christ and his mother, together with his disciples. There the infant Saviour lay in his cradle. We also saw him on the cross, with blood and water flowing from his side,—a picture which, to those who believe, causes serious reflections. Again, we saw him in the tomb, to rise a conquering God as he was.

In the Main Building (Argentine Republic) were many mummies that had been prepared in their own land, after the custom of that people to dispose of their dead. They were horrible-looking objects, in almost all positions, some sitting, others standing with their dresses on,—which were very rude, looking like so many rags and cords that age had nearly consumed,—which made them look the more unpleasant.

There were also quantities of soap, rock salt, saltpetre, yarns, woven goods, vegetable and mineral materials, pottery and glass, furniture, and many objects of general use. Clothing, ornaments, travelling equipments and carriages, vehicles of very odd-looking structure, all of which I must acknowledge I was much amused at.

To one who had never travelled in foreign lands it was a great privilege indeed to see the whole world come together, each vying to outdo the other. I hardly know how to estimate so great a privilege. To see so much, or nearly the skill and products of almost the whole world, for a few dollars, and sleep in one's bed every night, instead of being subjected to the indignity of others!

There was one thing I was constrained to observe, and that was the quiet demeanor of the people that were visiting the place. Although there were many thousands congregated at the same time, you did not hear a profane word, or see any misbehavior. Another thing I noticed was, that in a whole day you would scarce see any one whom you knew. All faces seemed strange, and all seemed bent on the one object, to see the world, or things thereof, whilst it was all together. The displays were grand beyond expression, and all seemed to enjoy it. As to my own part, I was completely absorbed, so much so that I became oblivious to all things else.

In the Main Building I think that almost all nations were represented.

Great Britain, through which I had the pleasure to pass and observe her mineral ores and mining products, together with her ten thousand other things.

New Zealand, with minerals and mining products.

Victoria, minerals, star antimony, clay, polished marble, geological specimens, etc.

New South Wales, specimens of gold, iron, fossils, government printing-office, tin, ingots of copper.

Bahamas, mining products and building stone.

Bermudas, about the same as above.

Queensland, flag-stone, coal, gold in nuggets, plumbago.

Tasmania, gold in quartz, asbestos, tin, coal.

Canada, France, Germany, Austria, Switzerland, Belgium, Netherlands, Denmark, Sweden, Norway,

Italy, Egypt, and many other countries too tedious
to enumerate, all of whose wares and products I
had the pleasant satisfaction to pass through and
see. I think the sight was perfectly invigorating.
I returned home every time feeling better at night
than when I went in the morning.

As I have only spoken of old countries, I must
say a word about the United States, or some of
their exhibits. As I have not much time or space,
I shall be very brief, with a hope that I shall have
time to return to it again.

I will begin at New York, Tiffany & Co., jew-
elry. I had the pleasure to see some of their large
and splendid diamonds and necklaces, which were
rare curiosities. I think one of these diamond
necklaces was valued at one hundred and eleven
thousand dollars, and I wish the reader to know
that I did not purchase them.

From this I go to Machinery Hall. On entering you are at once attracted by that mammoth
Corliss engine, laboring as though he intended to
show the people that he could, or was able to, set
the whole world in motion. Like a mighty giant,
he stood firm in the centre of his more diminutive
fellows only to command, and they as readily to

obey. When he moved they all moved in harmony with him. He reminded me of the leviathan in Job, forty-first chapter: "There is none like him upon the earth." It was wonderful, indeed, to see all the minor machines driven by the one, and all performing different branches of manufacturing, such as weaving, spinning, knitting, candy-making, paper-making, printing, and almost ten thousand other things to attract and surprise the beholder.

In this hall, also, all nations were represented with their various products of art and manufacture and engines of war. There was the Krupp gun, a most formidable-looking life-destroyer. I was curious enough to wonder where the man lived that was so ingenious to provide something of such magnitude for the peace and happiness of mankind, and for the prolongation of life.

We also saw the diving-bell, made for descending into the deep water for the purpose of reclaiming lost treasure that had been swept overboard from ships. This bell has been successfully used in many instances.

Helmets, such as the ancient soldiers used to protect themselves with in battle against their enemies, were also on exhibition.

CHAPTER XXIX.

We will now go to the Government Building, where we are as much astonished as before to see the thousands of models of all kinds of machinery. Here you get an idea of the inventive faculty of man. Here, too, the Stone Age is largely represented. Indian relics are in great abundance,—their war implements and cooking apparatus. We are caused to wonder how they succeed with such rude implements.

There was one thing of Indian manufacture that attracted my attention as much as anything else, and that was a boat, sixty feet long and eight feet wide, hewn out of a solid tree.

What kind of tools they used to accomplish their object I did not learn. At any rate, it was a wonderful tree and a wonderful work.

There were fishes and almost all kinds of animals that had been prepared by skilful taxidermists, whales of different specimens, bears of different kinds, and a great many small animals. As to war implements, they were in great profusion,—guns of all kinds, large and small.

I had the pleasure to see the fixtures of General Washington's house, cooking-utensils, andirons, shovel, tongs, muskets and swords, and several of his coats, vests, and pants; also his camp-chest and writing-apparatus.

We will now pass on to the Art Gallery. As I was not much of an artist it did not seem so interesting to me, although I saw some very fine works of art which could not fail to interest the visitor. There were many paintings from nearly all countries, and fine sculptures, but I was not able to judge which nation should carry off the palm.

Thence we went to the Agricultural Building, and there I felt more at home. Here were a great number of agricultural machines in operation, comprising everything used in tillage or harvesting, most of which I had some conception of. Manufactured food, and fish of all varieties, with which I was much delighted.

Next we entered Horticultural Hall, and here we were delighted with the beauty and curiosity of the tropical plants and almost every variety of garden decoration.

After getting through the five principal buildings, we then go indiscriminately from place to place. I will not leave the New England farmhouse out of remembrance. It was built of logs in the style of one hundred years ago, and was very familiar to me, as I had seen such in my boyhood, in New Jersey, fifty years ago.

The inmates of this house were dressed in the old-fashioned style, and had the old-fashioned bonnets hung upon nails all-around the house. The little spinning-wheel was standing on the floor in the room, a chicken was suspended before the old-fashioned fireplace to roast. Some of the women were knitting, and others sewing patchwork. Everything seemed to be carried on as systematically as if these same people had lived there for a hundred years.

We then passed into the Colorado State Building, and there saw wonderful exhibits of minerals, vegetable products, and also very fine specimens of their skill in taxidermy, said to be done by a lady, whose name has now escaped my memory.

It was a splendid scene to the beholder, and impressed one with the idea that Americans are a progressive people, and that they have made great advancement in the first one hundred years of their existence, and we might almost conclude that they had already arrived at the height of perfection. Admitting that there is much chance for improvement and advancement, I do not see how it can be possible, even in a hundred years to come, to surpass the present as far as two does one.

I also had the pleasure to pass through the Swedish school-house, and viewed with astonishment their educational systems, methods, libraries, maps, and drawings, and many works by pupils. I also visited the Annex to the Main Building, and there I beheld that mysterious gorilla, captured by whom I did not learn. It was a most formidable-looking creature, having some resemblance to the human being. I think it was between five and six feet high, very broad across the chest, the legs shorter in proportion than those of a man; the arms, reaching nearly to the knees, appeared to be formed for walking on the ground. The skin seemed to be black in color, and covered with dark gray hair; on the head this was of a darkish brown. The hair was longest on the arms. The face hairy, but the chest bare; the mouth large and wide, neck very short. It looked, on the whole, like something to be dreaded either by man or beast, and I regret that I cannot give a better description of it.

In the Main Building Annex also were a great quantity of medicines and medicinal plants and roots from China. A large quantity of China work, statues of male and female dressed gaudily, the ladies having the small feet we have so often read about. In this building was a large quantity of mineral ores of various kinds from the various parts of the world.

I visited Cook's ticket-office, and there saw the Egyptian princess who had lived, it is said, three thousand years ago. We can only say that the body is still with us to look upon, but where the departed spirit is is unknown.

It is wonderful to keep a lifeless body three thousand years on the earth, to be looked upon and carried from place to place to be exhibited, to show a skill in the art of embalming unknown to us.

As we travelled around among the little booths we saw many persons from foreign lands, some said to be from Egypt, selling various kinds of trinkets, many of which were said to be made of wood from the Mount of Olives. Some were small pieces of wood planed, which they were selling at high prices. It was a marvel to me that those people understood extortion so well; it seems to me that all men are brothers in that particular. All salesmen like the advantage, even if the purchaser is duped.

I spent thirteen days at the Centennial Exhibition with much gratification. I always went home exhilarated, musing over what I had seen in the world of wonders. From the beginning I made it a particular point to be there every other Friday, never missing one day that I appointed. It seemed to me that every day I went was fair and pleasant, with one or two exceptions.

I have only to regret that I am not able to give a full history of the Centennial Exhibition. I have only written from memory, not having time to take notes whilst I was visiting this great world of wonders.

I must now leave off this imperfect sketch, and

congratulate myself on having seen the first Centennial of the United States of America. I do not know the child at present born who may live to see the next one.

This world is not our home, and should we be possessors of all that we have seen with our eyes, with all its charms and glittering show, we are admonished that we must leave for other spheres of which we have not yet made the acquaintance; a country where I hope our eyes will not tire of seeing, or our bodies be wearied; a land where the inhabitant shall no more say, " I am sick."

IN MEMORY OF D. SPENCER BATES.

BY J. STILL.

Adieu, adieu, my parents dear,
I go away and leave you here;
I will enlist, the Southern foe to quell,—
The rights of the North to me are dear.
Adieu, adieu, my brothers and sisters all,
Like strings you twine around my heart;
But I'll obey the National call,
And with its army act my part.
I'll bear the heat, endure the toil;
I'll travel south to meet the foe;
I'll rush with vigor to the battle-field;
We only live for Freedom here below.
Should I fail and fall, grieve not for me,
It is the duty of us all to fight for liberty.
I trust that God will bless
My aged parents dear;
And be a comfort and a staff
In their declining years.

Should sickness o'ertake me, whilst thus so far away,
My parents dear will not be there,
To comfort and give water,
And speak a word of cheer;
But oh! I'll grasp the hand of a stranger
Whilst these sufferings I endure.

My days are almost ended,
And I shall fight no more;
I'll send a little book unto my native home,—
Read it, brothers, read it, sisters,—
It's the last you'll have from me;
For I am sinking, I am sinking into eternity.

Scorching fevers now have seized me,
Death is staring in my face;
Come, O God! Oh, come and save me,
And take me to Thyself.

Weep not for me, my dearest mother,
When you view my last remains;
A metallic coffin doth surround me,—
It's nought to Slavery's chains.

Whilst friends stand weeping all around,
And wring their hands in vain,
My soul hath fled to God who gave it,
And never will return.

Ah! mothers, you have sons most dear
Enlisted in this sad war of ours;
Dry up your tears, and tell your fears,
It is the Nation's downfall.

THE BEREAVED FAMILY.

BY JAMES STILL.

Whilst sitting chatting in the family circle,
  The father and the mother too were there;
The sons and daughters little thinking
  Of the fate their mother soon should share.

When lo! at once an unseen messenger arrived,
  And to the mother he was an unwelcome guest,
And with his dart he touched her heart;
  Her head fell on her breast.

" What's the matter?" exclaimed the father,
  " Mother, are you fainting?" says the son;
" Perhaps a fit," said a daughter,
  " For a doctor you must run!"

But lo! her voice is hushed for ever,
  Never to be heard again;
Father and children, they are grieving,
  Death their beloved one has slain.

268

" Oh !" exclaimed the daughters,
  " Our mother is slain, and gone
Without one moment's warning,
  Oh ! mother, speak again."

But lo ! a solemn silence ;
  A lifeless lump of clay,
Prostrate on the cooling board
  Their mother had to lay.

Ten thousand thousand tears are shed,
  Around their mother dear,
But still the grave must be her bed,
  She is no longer here.

The silent messenger that came,
  No eye has seen, no ear has heard ;
He did fulfil his mission soon,
  And bore the mother to another world.

Nothing on earth the daughters want ;
  The sons would like to die ;
Their father grieves, his love is gone,
  She's in eternity.

No more to meet again around the family board,
  Where their dear mother was to them their all ;
She's with departed spirits,
  And never will return.

When taking the last farewell of their departed mother,
   A voice, from a daughter, said,
" Mother! mother! mother!"
   On each living ear with horror fell.

" Oh, can I longer live?"
   Exclaimed a weeping son;
" If all this world was mine, I'd give it
   If my mother could return."

We little thought of this
   A few days ago,
All was joy and happiness,
   Now it's sadness, grief, and woe.

A mother's fondest care
   In a moment may be severed,
By death's fatal quiver,
   But still may be remembered.

On this twelfth day of March,
   In eighteen fifty-four,
We to the silent tomb
   Our lovely mother bore.

There were sad lamentations,
   And bitter weeping, too,
Deep sighs and faintings
   Among the living crew.

They formed a long procession,
　　One mile in length;
And many hearts were gloomy,
　　The daughters still were faint.

And as they drove along
　　Towards the silent tomb,
The children screamed and cried,
　　They knew not what to do.

And at the grave a voice
　　Both calm and loud was heard;
It cried lowly for mother,
　　No mother's voice was heard.

They then returned home,
　　All gloomy, sad, and dreary;
The night came on, they had to mourn,
　　No mother to be with them.

They lived a happy circle
　　Before they separated,
The father and the children
　　Would all consult with mother.

Let what would be wanted,
　　They would to mother go;
But now the tune is turned,
　　They can't to mother go.

They wrung their hands and cried,
    Their hearts throbbed quick and heavy,
Their all to them had died,
    No mother to be with them.

Like Esther of old,
    She was noble, just, and true;
And in her family circle
    Like her there were but few.

Just on the very spot
    That first gave her birth,
There time with her did end,
    And she's prepared for earth.

Her aged mother, too, was there,
    Who did that daughter bear,
Her briny tears did fall;
    She was once a mother's care.

THE OTHER LAND.

BY JAMES STILL.

Through this dark wilderness
  We all must travel on,
To a land unseen by mortal eyes,
  Where many thousands have gone.

Beyond this vale there is a land,
  Where night is changed to day,
Nothing there to mar our peace,
  Or clouds to pass away.

A happy home where the good may rest,
  No sorrow there may come,
For tears are wiped from every eye,
  In that heavenly, happy home.

No sorrow there, or crying heard,
  Joy is the crown all wear,
Robed in linen clean and white,
  While conquering palms they bear.

There candles we shall never need
　　To light our path along,
The Lamb himself is the light thereof,
　　The theme of harp and song.

The streets are of transparent gold,
　　Rivers of life do flow,
Where all may drink and drink again,
　　Till they God's fulness know.

THE END.

Index